THE GAZE

A Commentary on
Divine and Human Mercy

RANIERO CANTALAMESSA

Translated by Marsha Daigle-Williamson, PhD

To His Holiness Pope Francis,
who has placed mercy at the center
of the life and reflection of the Church.

English language edition © 2015 by Raniero Cantalamessa
First published in Italian by Edizioni San Paolo s.r.l.
Piazza Soncino 5 – 20092 Cinisello Balsamo
Milan, Italy, © 2015 by Edizioni San Paolo, s.rl.

Published by The Word Among Us Press
7115 Guilford Drive
Frederick, Maryland 21704
www.wau.org

19 18 17 16 15   1 2 3 4 5
ISBN: 978-1-59325-285-4
eISBN: 978-1-59325-477-3

Scripture texts used in this work are taken from The Catholic
Edition of Revised Standard Version Bible, copyright © 1965, 1966
by the Division of Christian Education of the National Council of
the Churches of Christ in the United States of America. Used with
permission. All rights reserved.

Cover design by Faceout Studios
Cover image: Georges Rouault(1871–1958), *The Head of Christ*
@ 2015 Artists Rights Society (ARS), New York / ADAGP, Paris
Photo image @ The Cleveland Museum of Art

Library of Congress Control Number: 2015953884

TABLE OF CONTENTS

INTRODUCTION

I read the statement somewhere (I can't remember where) that "Too many discussions about love circle around its mystery rather than entering into it." I believe the same must be said about mercy, which is a particular aspect of love. The discussion that I am about to present belongs to the first category and circles around the mystery of mercy. To enter into the mystery, we need to be attracted to it. One can knock at the door, but the door can only be opened from the inside. The mystery of mercy is in fact identified in the Bible with the pure and simple mystery of God. It is the burning bush that one cannot approach without our sandals being removed, that is, without having abandoned the pretense of moving ahead on our own with our own arguments.

So why, then, write about mercy? The question is a real one. What helped me to get beyond it is the memory of a Gospel episode, the episode of the paralytic narrated by the Gospel writer John, who was at the pool of Bethsaida for thirty-eight years (see John 5:1ff). People believed that the water in the pool had the power to heal the first person who plunged into it when an angel stirred the water. The unfortunate man complained to Jesus that he had no one to lower him into the water at just the right time.

The pool worked the miracle, but it was necessary for someone to help the paralytic get in it, to plunge him into it. This is the goal and the hope that make me venture to write these pages: to encourage and "push" myself as I write to leap into the great healing pool of God's mercy—and, if possible, those who would read this book. Its waters are once again being "stirred" for a whole year, thanks to the Jubilee Year of Mercy called by Pope Francis on the occasion of the fiftieth anniversary of the Second Vatican Council.

The link between the theme of mercy and the Second Vatican Council is anything but arbitrary or minor. St. John XXIII, in his opening address for the council on October 11, 1962, pointed to mercy as the new approach in the council's style: "The Church has always opposed . . . errors [throughout the ages]. Frequently she has condemned them with the greatest severity. Nowadays, however, the Spouse of Christ prefers to make use of the medicine of mercy rather than that of severity."[1] In a certain sense, half a century later the Year of Mercy celebrates the faithfulness of the Church to this promise.

A comment on this book's contents. The word "mercy" (*hesed* in Hebrew, *eleos* in Greek) recurs in the Old Testament and the New Testament in two contexts and with two different meanings, even though they are interdependent. Its first and original meaning indicates the sentiment that God fosters toward human beings. Its second meaning indicates the sentiment that human beings should

---

[1] www.vatican2voice.org/91docs/opening_speech.htm. All quotes from papal and council documents in this book are from the Vatican website.

foster toward one another: mercy as a *gift* and mercy as a *duty,* or rather, as we will see, as a *debt*.

Consequently, in the first part of the book, we will reflect on God's mercy, on its manifestations in the history of salvation and in Christ and on the means of grace in the Church's sacraments through which mercy reaches us. In the second part, we will reflect on our duty to be merciful and on the "works" of mercy, in particular on the duty of the Church and its ministers to be merciful to sinners, just as Jesus was.

It has been rightly said about Orthodox icons that the body is included for the sake of the face, and the face is included as a frame for the gaze. That is the reason for the choice of the book's title and for the cover image. It is rare to find an image that speaks to us of the merciful gaze of Christ with more power than this face of Christ by Georges Rouault.

Chapter 1

In the Beginning Was Love
(Not Mercy!)

1. God Is Love

John begins his Gospel by saying, "In the beginning was the Word" (John 1:1). He does not say "the beginning was the Word," but *in* the beginning was the Word. The Word "was in the beginning with God" (1:2) but was not itself "the beginning." The beginning of everything is not the Word or an abstract divine essence or a Supreme Being but the Person of the Father.

According to the traditional view of the Greek Fathers, which is increasingly more widely shared by Latin theology today, the concept of unity in God is not separable from the concept of the Trinity but forms a unique mystery and flows from a unique act. With our limited human vocabulary, we can say that the Father is the fountain, the absolute origin, of the movement of love. The Son cannot exist as the Son unless he receives from the Father all that he is. The Father is the only one, even within the Trinity, who does not need to be loved in order to love.

The unique God of the Christians is thus the Father—not, however, conceived of on his own (how can he be called "father" unless he has a son?), but as the Father always begetting the Son and giving himself to him with an infinite love that unites them both, which is the Holy Spirit.

This love in the Trinity, which constitutes the Trinity, is their very *nature*, to use a word accessible to us even if it is inadequate; it is not *grace*. It is love, not mercy. The Father loving the Son is not a grace or a concession; it is in a certain sense a necessity. The Father needs to love in order to exist as Father. The Son loving the Father is not a concession or a grace; it is an intrinsic necessity even if it occurs with the utmost freedom; the Son needs to be loved and to love in order to be the Son. The Father begets the Son in the Holy Spirit by *loving him*; the Father and the Son breathe forth the Holy Spirit in *loving each other*.

What St. Bernard says about love is fully and absolutely realized only in God; it has no other "why" outside itself: "Love suffices in itself; it pleases in itself and for its own sake. It is its own merit and reward. Love does not need any cause beyond itself, nor any fruit—its fruit is its use. I love because I love; I love so that I may love."[2] Love is enough unto itself, but nothing is enough for love! The action of God toward human beings is proof of that!

---

[2] St. Bernard, On the Song of Songs, "Sermon 83," 4, quoted in Bernard McGinn, *The Essential Writings of Christian Mysticism* (New York: Modern Library, 2006), p. 259; see *Opera omnia*, ed. Cisterc. 2, 1958, pp. 300–301.

2. Love Makes a Gift of Itself

What happens when God created the world and human beings in it who are made in his image and likeness? Love makes a gift of itself. Love, like the good, by its nature "tends to pour itself out"; it is "*diffusivum sui.*"[3] In the fourth Eucharistic prayer in use after the Second Vatican Council, the Church prays, "[You] have made all that is, so that you might fill your creatures with blessings and bring joy to many of them by the glory of your light." St. Catherine of Siena, in one of her prayers, expressed this same truth with impassioned words:

> Why then, Eternal Father, did you create this creature of yours? I am truly amazed at this, and indeed I see, as you show me, that you made us for one reason only: in your light you saw yourself compelled by the fire of your charity to give us being, in spite of the evil we would commit against you, eternal Father. It was fire, then, that compelled you. O unutterable love, even though you saw all the evils that all your creatures would commit against your infinite goodness, you acted as if you did not see and set your eye only on the beauty of your creature, with whom you had fallen in love like one drunk and crazy with love. And in love you drew us out of yourself, giving us being in your own image and likeness.

---

[3] St. Thomas Aquinas, *Summa Theologiae* I, q. 5, a. 4, ad 2.

You, eternal Truth, have told me the truth: that love compelled you to create us.[4]

This love poured out is grace and no longer "love as God's nature"; it is gratuitous. It could not be otherwise and is thus a gift, a condescension. It is *hesed*, mercy. St. Irenaeus has a wonderful passage on this point:

> God did not accept . . . the friendship of Abraham, as though He stood in need of it, for He was perfect from the beginning . . . , but that He in His goodness might bestow eternal life upon Abraham himself, inasmuch as the friendship of God imparts immortality to those who embrace it. In the beginning did God form Adam, not as if He stood in need of men, but that he might have . . . [someone] upon whom to confer His benefits. . . . [Service] to God does indeed profit God nothing but He grants . . . benefits upon those who serve [Him] because they do serve Him, and on His followers because they do follow Him; but He does not receive any benefit from them: for He is rich, perfect, and in need of nothing.[5]

St. Catherine says that God was "compelled" by his love to create us, but St. Irenaeus seems to be saying the opposite. Both assertions express a truth about the mystery: God's creation of us

[4] Catherine of Siena, *The Prayers of Catherine of Siena*, ed. Suzanne Noffke (New York: Paulist Press, 1983), pp. 112–113.

[5] St. Irenaeus, *Irenaeus of Lyons: Against Heresies*, IV, 13, 4–4, 14, 1 (N. p.: Ex Fontibus, 2015), p. 415.

is a necessity, but it is also freely undertaken on his part; he is compelled by his love, yet his actions remain completely free.

The mercy of God thus predates humanity's sin; it is not just a response to sin because it exists prior to sin. It is through mercy (*eleos*), writes St. Athanasius, that God creates human beings "in his image" and endows them with reason (so they can recognize him) and with language (so they can praise him).[6] It is by grace and mercy that we are chosen in Christ "before the foundation of the world, . . . destined . . . to be his sons" (Ephesians 1:4-5).

3. The Gift Becomes Forgiveness

What does the fact of sin introduce into this picture that is new? In brief, mercy as a *gift* becomes mercy as *forgiveness*. The distinction that Nicholas Cabasilas, a Byzantine theologian in the thirteenth century, makes between love as a gift and love that suffers helps us understand this point:

> Two things reveal him who loves . . . one, that he in every possible way does good to the object of his love; the other, that he is willing, if need be, to endure terrible things for him and suffer pain. Of the two the latter would seem to be a far greater proof of friendship than the former. Yet it was not possible for God since He is

---

[6] See St. Athanasius, *On the Incarnation*, 3, 11, trans. and intro. John Behr (Yonkers, NY: St. Vladimir's Seminary, 2011), pp. 52, 60–61; see *PG* 25, 101, 116.

incapable of suffering harm. . . . So he devised this self-emptying and carried it out, and made the instrument [i.e., Christ's human nature] by which He might be able to endure terrible things and to suffer pain. When He had thus proved by the things which He endured that He indeed loves exceedingly, He turned man, who had fled from the Good One because he had believed himself to be the object of hate, towards Himself.[7]

People's sin and rebellion produce a wound in God: the love that was gift becomes a love that suffers. Cabasilas, as we see, delays the suffering love of God until the time of the Incarnation and passion of Christ. However, in the third century Origen had already expressed a different idea that is being rediscovered and welcomed today by theology and even by the magisterium of the Church. Origen writes,

[The Savior] came down to earth out of compassion for the human race. . . . [He] experienced our sufferings even before he suffered on the cross, before he condescended to assume our flesh: For if he had not suffered, he would not have come down to live on the level of human life. . . . What is this suffering that he suffered for us? It is the suffering of love. The Father, too, himself, the God of the universe, "patient and abounding in mercy" [Psalm 103:8] and

---

[7] Nicholas Cabasilas, *Life in Christ*, VI, 2, trans. Carmino J. deCatanzaro (Crestwood, NY: St. Vladimir's Seminary, 1974), p. 163; see *PG* 150, 645.

compassionate, does he not in some way suffer? Or do you not know that when he directs human affairs he suffers human suffering? . . . [He] suffers . . . [because] of love.[8]

Origen's insight had to wait for the great catastrophes of the last century to resurface to the consciousness of the Church. In the second half of the last century, some of the most noted theologians have spoken about the suffering of God, and the International Theological Commission has offered a substantially positive judgment on their readings.[9] This perspective, with the necessary qualifications and cautions, was accepted by John Paul II who wrote this in his encyclical on the Holy Spirit:

The concept of God as the necessarily most perfect being certainly excludes from God any pain deriving from deficiencies or wounds; but in the "depths of God" there is a Father's love that, faced with man's sin, in the language of the Bible reacts so deeply as to say: "I am sorry that I have made him" [cf. Genesis 6:7]. . . . But more often the Sacred Book speaks to us of a Father who feels compassion for man, as though sharing his pain. In a word, this inscrutable and indescribable fatherly "pain" will bring about above all the wonderful economy of redemptive love in Jesus Christ, so that

---

[8] Origen, "Homily 6," 6, in *Origen: Homilies 1–14 on Ezekiel*, trans. and intro. Thomas P. Scheck (Mahwah, NJ: Paulist Press, 2010), pp. 92–93; see *GCS* 1925, p. 384; see also Origen's *Commentary on Matthew* 10, 23, *GCS* 1935, p. 33.

[9] See "Teologia, cristologia, antropologia," in *Civiltà Cattolica*, 1983, pp. 50–65.

through the *mysterium pietatis* love can reveal itself in the history of man as stronger than sin. . . . Jesus [is] the Redeemer, in whose humanity the "suffering" of God is concretized.[10]

There is no new idea here but rather the recovery of the true face of God in the Bible that was obscured for centuries by the idea of "the God of the philosophers," an unmovable mover who moves everything without himself moving—much less *being moved* by anything. A Jewish rabbi came to the same conclusion as Christian theologians just by studying and commenting on the Bible. Even before today's theologians mentioned above, he wrote, "Does God suffer? This is a terrible question. . . . It seems to me that God is wounded; God suffers in His justice or in His mercy [that is, when he punishes sin or when he overlooks sin]. He suffers because of the man who sins, He suffers with the man who sins."[11]

When we speak of the suffering of God, we should not focus unilaterally on the Father's suffering but on the suffering of all three divine Persons. The suffering of God is trinitarian! The Holy Spirit himself, being the love of God in person, is also consequently "God's pain in person."[12]

---

[10] *Dominum et vivificantem* [On the Holy Spirit in the Life of the Church and the World], n. 39.

[11] Eugenio Zolli, *Before the Dawn: Autobiographical Reflections* (1954; repr. ed., San Francisco: Ignatius Press, 2008), pp. 31–32.

[12] See Heribert Mühlen, "Das Herz Gottes: Neue Aspekte der Trinitätslehre, " in "*Theologie und Glaube*, 78 (1988): 141–159.

What reconciles the discussion of God's suffering with our unshakable faith in his perfection and power is that love will triumph in the end over every kind of pain. Then "he will wipe away every tear from their eyes, and death shall be no more, neither shall there be mourning nor crying nor pain any more" (Revelation 21:4)—either for us or for God. Love will triumph, but in its own way: not by destroying evil and turning it back beyond our borders (that cannot be done without destroying human freedom) but by converting evil into good, hate into love.

4. The "Visceral" Love of God

To understand something about God's suffering, we need to take into account the distinction between nature and person in the Trinity. In terms of his nature, God is omnipotent and absolutely perfect; there cannot be any pain in him deriving from a loss of vitality because he is the Living One who gives life to everything and never undergoes any loss of life. Thus, when we say that there cannot be any pain in God, we are speaking of his nature. The Father is a person who possesses a divine nature and, as such, concretely expresses his personality in a series of interpersonal relationships with the Son and the Spirit but also with human beings and the angels he created. In the first category of relationships intrinsic to his intimate life with the Son and the Spirit, any kind of pain is absent. Their perfect unity of love and life excludes every form of pain.

However, the Father is not only the Father of the Son and the fountainhead of the Spirit but also the creator of the world and the human beings he placed in charge of it. He freely entered into a relationship of love and communion with human beings in the image of the relationship he has with the Son. He enters into this relationship with all his glory and all his love. The bond the Father has with the world, then, involves the inner depths of his whole personality. This is the relationship in which pain occurs for him.

The Father's plan for creation cannot actually come to pass without the collaboration and free adherence of human beings. In saying no to God, human beings strike at the very heart of the three divine Persons and their desire for a communion of love with human beings. This is the source of their pain, the refusal of human beings to be involved in their love and their holiness. Pain, as we see, is not a lessening or loss of life in God but is only a modality through which he expresses his fullness of life and love in the face of the rejection by human beings.

What happens in God is comparable to what takes place in a woman who has an intense desire for motherhood but who, for physical reasons or her husband's refusal, cannot become a mother. The frustration of her vivid desire for maternity causes her inner agony! In the same way, the refusal of obedience and of love on the part of human beings blocks God's very intense desire to make human beings partners in his glory.

The previous comparison helps us understand some of the most beautiful and powerful texts from the Old Testament on God's mercy. The reaction of God to the unfaithfulness of his people is compared in those texts to the visceral sentiment of love-pain that a woman experiences with the rebellion or disgrace of her offspring: "Is Ephraim my dear son? / Is he my darling child? / For as often as I speak against him, / I do remember him still. / Therefore my heart yearns for him; / I will surely have mercy on him, says the LORD" (Jeremiah 31:20).

The word that is translated as "heart," "innermost being," or "viscera" is *rahamim* in Hebrew. It comes from *rehem*, which means a mother's womb. This is a painful love, like the one that Jeremiah himself experiences during the imminent misfortune that is about to fall upon his people:

> My anguish, my anguish [also translated as "heart" or "bowels"]!
> I writhe in pain!
> Oh, the walls of my heart!
> My heart is beating wildly;
> I cannot keep silent;
> for I hear the sound of the trumpet,
> the alarm of war. (Jeremiah 4:19)

It is as though God accepts taking upon himself the suffering due to the consequences of his people's sin, announcing beforehand what will in fact take place on the cross. We read in Hosea that the people are hard to convert: the more God draws the people to himself, the more they do not understand and turn to idols. What should God do in this situation? Abandon them? Destroy them? Through the prophet, God is sharing his own inner drama that demonstrates a kind of "weakness" and impotence due to his passionate love for human beings. God experiences his "heart skip a beat" at the thought that his people could be destroyed:

> My heart recoils [is turned from anger to pity] within me,
>   my compassion grows warm and tender.
> I will not execute my fierce anger . . .
> for I am God and not man. (Hosea 11:8-9)

A human being in similar circumstances could give vent to the heat of his anger and normally does so, but God, because he is "holy," is different. Even if we are unfaithful, he remains faithful because he cannot deny himself (see 2 Timothy 2:13). God finds himself without any coercive or defensive ability before human beings. If human beings choose to block his creative act of love within them, he does not intervene to impose his authority on them. He can only infinitely respect the free choice of human beings. They can reject him and eliminate him from their lives, and he will let them do that and not defend himself. Or better, his way of defending himself and defending human beings against their own destruction will be to continue to love, and to do so eternally.

This is "the pool," or better, the depths of the mystery that is open before us. All we need to do is immerse ourselves into it with amazement and gratitude.

CHAPTER 2

"In remembrance of his mercy"
THE MERCY OF GOD BECOMES FLESH

1. The Innovation of the Incarnation

The Gospel opens with a kind of canticle about God's mercy from many voices. This is the way the so-called infancy Gospel of Luke begins. Mary, in the Magnificat, sings of the mercy (*eleos*) of God that extends "from generation to generation." She says God has acted "in remembrance of his mercy, / as he spoke to our fathers, / to Abraham and to his posterity for ever" (Luke 1:50, 54-55). Zechariah does the same in his canticle. He says that God has performed "the mercy promised to our fathers" and has "remember[ed] his holy covenant" (1:72). He goes on to say that "through the tender mercy of our God [literally the "viscera of mercy"], / the dayspring has visited us from on high" (1:78).

To understand the significance of the innovation in all these expressions, we need to be aware of what devout Israelites were waiting for and what they were praying to God for during the time preceding the coming of Christ. Fortunately, we have one of these prayers in Sirach 36:1-17:

Lift up thy hand. . . .
Show signs anew, and work further wonders. . . .

Hasten the day, and remember the appointed time,

and let people recount thy mighty deeds. . . .

Have mercy, O Lord, upon the people called by thy name,

upon Israel. . . .

and fulfil the prophecies spoken in thy name. (Sirach 36:3, 6,
8, 12, 15)

At one time people said, "Lift up thy hand," but now Mary says,
"He has shown strength with his arm." The people said, "Work
further wonders," but now she says, "He who is mighty has done
great things." They said, "Remember!" and now, "He has remembered." The people said, "Have mercy on your people," and now,
"He has helped his servant Israel." They said, "Fulfil the prophecies," and now, "He has fulfilled the prophecies." This simple
change in verb tenses expresses a seismic shift, a movement from
the time of waiting to that of fulfillment, the actualization of the
eschatological event.

But where is the novelty, given that the Old Testament had
already said such fervent and touching things about the mercy of
God? The answer is found in the beginning of the Letter to the
Hebrews: "In many and various ways God spoke of old to our
fathers by the prophets; but in these last days he has spoken to us
by a Son" (Hebrews 1:1-2). God, who often spoke of his mercy
through a wonderful variety of prophetic voices, now speaks to
us "by a Son"; he no longer speaks through a go-between but "in

person," because the Son is the reflection of "the glory of God and bears the very stamp of his nature" (1:3).

The reality turns out to be even better than the parable of the merciful father. In the parable, the older son stays at home and actually resents the return of the younger son. But in the real-world application of the parable, the older brother (Jesus) himself has gone in search of the brother who had gone astray and has led him back to the Father. The only-begotten Son of God likewise descended "into a far country" (Luke 15:13), but in this case it was to bring back to the Father "the children of God who are scattered abroad" (John 11:52).

The Son not only "speaks" to us about God's mercy but is himself that mercy made flesh. A very ancient author paraphrased John 1:14 this way: "The love [of the Father] was made flesh in him."[13] Prior to any *act* of mercy on Christ's part and his telling of the parables on mercy, there is the *event* of mercy, the Incarnation. To the person who wondered what the Word brought that was new when he came to earth, St. Irenaeus answered that Christ "brought all . . . novelty by bringing himself."[14] It is indeed true; he himself was the great innovation, his becoming man.

---

[13] *The Gospel of Truth*, 23, one of the apocryphal gospels discovered at Nag Hammadi and included in the Nag Hammadi codices.
[14] Irenaeus of Lyons, *Against Heresies*, IV, 34, 1, p. 498.

2. Divine Condescension

Let us see in what sense the Incarnation of the Word constitutes the fundamental event of God's mercy. St. Augustine writes, "Could there be more mercy shown to us unhappy creatures than the mercy that induced the creator of heaven to descend from heaven and the creator of the earth to clothe himself with a mortal body? In eternity he remains equal to the Father but he made himself equal to us in our mortal nature. That same mercy led the Lord of the world to clothe himself in the nature of a servant." [15]

For St. Irenaeus, "the lost sheep" in Luke's parable is all of humanity represented by the fallen Adam, and the Incarnation is the moment in which Christ goes to find it and bring it back to the sheepfold on his shoulders. [16] Various Fathers of the Church gave not only a metaphoric but also a metaphysical meaning to this image. According to them, by becoming incarnate, the Word not only took on an individual human nature, but he also, in a certain sense, took on the whole of human nature conceived of as a concrete universal in the Platonic manner. Christian salvation, according to this view that was important to many Greek Fathers, is already completely realized in seed-form at the moment

---

[15] *Sermon* 207, *PL* 38, p. 1043.
[16] See Irenaeus of Lyons, *Against Heresies*, III, 23, 1, p. 361. This text from Irenaeus inspired Marko Rupnik's image of Jesus carrying the old Adam on his shoulders that was chosen as the logo for the Jubilee Year of Mercy.

in which the Son of God took on human flesh and inserted the seed of immortality into it.

There is still another respect in which the Incarnation is the definitive actualization of the mercy of God. When Moses prayed, "Show me thy glory" (Exodus 33:18), God answered, "'You cannot see my face; for man shall not see me and live.' And the LORD said, 'Behold, there is a place by me where you shall stand upon the rock; and while my glory passes by I will put you in a cleft of the rock, and I will cover you with my hand until I have passed by; then I will take away my hand, and you shall see my back; but my face shall not be seen'" (33:20-23). With the Incarnation God veiled his face so that people could see it and not die. God reveals himself by veiling himself. This is why John, after saying, "The Word became flesh," could exclaim, "We have beheld his glory!" (John 1:14). The Greek Fathers expressed this aspect of God's mercy with the word "*synkatabasis*," which means "condescension."[17] A third-century writing on this issue attributed to Pope Clement says,

For I maintain that the eyes of mortals cannot see the incorporeal form of the Father or Son, because it is illumined by exceeding great light. Wherefore it is not because God envies, but because He pities, that He cannot be seen by man who has been turned into flesh. For he who sees God cannot live. For the excess of light

---

[17] See St. John Chrysostom, *On the Incomprehensible Nature of God*, trans. Paul W. Harkins, vol. 72, Fathers of the Church (Washington, DC: Catholic University of America Press, 1984); see *SCh* 28, p. 176.

dissolves the flesh of him who sees; unless by the secret power of God the flesh be changed into the nature of light, so that it can see light, or the substance of light be changed into flesh, so that it can be seen by flesh.[18]

The Incarnation has brought this second supposition to pass.

3. The Pyramid Has Been Turned Upside Down

People have always conceived of the ascent to God as climbing a pyramid, trying to reach the pinnacle by their own intellectual or ascetic efforts. But they have done so in vain. Jesus says to Nicodemus, "No one has ascended into heaven but he who descended from heaven, the Son of man" (John 3:13). In becoming incarnate, God has reversed the path up that pyramid: he is at its base now; he has picked us up and now carries us on his shoulders, so to speak, just like the shepherd with the lost sheep. We can reach him now because he first came to us.

The dominant perception of God among educated people during the time of the New Testament was the so-called God of the philosophers. Plato asserted that "Gods do not mix with men,"[19] and

---

[18] Pseudo-Clementine, "Homily 17," 16, in Pseudo-Clementine Literature, vol. 8, Ante-Nicene Fathers, ed. Philip Schaff (New York: Christian Literature Publishing, 1886), pp. 322–323; see PG 2, 400 A.

[19] Plato, Symposium, 203a, trans. and intro. Alexander Nehamas and Paul Woodruff (Indianapolis: Hackett, 1989), p. 47.

Aristotle said that God "moves [the universe] by being loved [not because he loves!]."[20] The religious notion of imitating God, the idea of "our assimilation to God as far as we can,"[21] arose from this view of God.

With the Incarnation, God has completely reversed this ideal. "In this is love, not that we loved God but that he loved us and sent his Son to be the expiation for our sins. . . . We love, because he first loved us" (1 John 4:10, 19). The poet Charles Péguy has expressed this idea in his very distinct style (in which he has God speak in the first person):

"People are always talking," says God, "about the imitation
   of Jesus Christ
Which is the imitation, the faithful imitation of my Son
   by human beings. . . .
But in the end we must not forget
That my Son began with his own unique imitation of man.
Completely faithful to it.
He pushed it to a perfect identification with man
When he so faithfully and so perfectly took on
   the human condition. . . .

---

[20] *Metaphysics* XII, 7, 1072b, *Aristotle's "Metaphysics,"* trans. John Warrington (New York: E. P. Dutton, 1956), p. 345.
[21] Plato, *Theaetetus Reading Plato's "Theaetetus,"* trans. and comm. Timothy Chappell (Indianapolis: Hackett, 1989), p. 225; see also Plotinus, *Enneads*, I, 2, 4; I, 6, 6.

In suffering.

In living.

In dying."[22]

Before the imitation of God by human beings, there was first the imitation of man by God.

The pyramid, as I said, was turned upside down once and for all when the Word became flesh. Now, however, it needs to be reversed inside of us as well. The pyramid, once turned upside down, always tends, unfortunately, because of sin and presumption, to return to its former default position. By birth and by our tendency to regress, we all belong to that same human race that thought it could reach God and obtain his grace with our own works and ideas. We belong to the same category of people (in the Gospels, the Pharisees) about whom Paul sadly noted that they were "ignorant of the righteousness that comes from God, and [sought] to establish their own" (Romans 10:3). In other words, we think that we can save ourselves through our own works. St. Augustine in his *Confessions* reveals how difficult it was for him to reach the reversal achieved by the Incarnation: "I was not humble enough to cleave to him who is humble."[23]

---

[22] Charles Péguy, *Le Mystère des Saints Innocents*, in *Oeuvres poétiques complètes* (Paris: Gallimard, 1957), p. 692.

[23] St Augustine, *Confessions*, VII, 18, vol. 1, trans. and ed. Carolyn J. B. Hammond (Cambridge, MA: Harvard University Press, 2014), p. 341.

Is it a mistake, then, to want to "reach up toward God"? Is St. Bonaventure on the wrong track when he writes *The Journey of the Mind to God,* conceiving of it as an ascent to God through the vestiges of God that remain in our nature and in ourselves? No, and for a very good reason. The ascent now takes place with Christ, as we follow behind him. Bonaventure's treatise ends with Jesus who, through the passover of his death and resurrection, has reopened the path for us to rise up to heaven with him.[24]

The Christian philosopher Søren Kierkegaard has a very beautiful prayer about God loving us first. Let us make it our prayer at the end of this meditation on God's mercy in the Incarnation:

You have loved us *first*, O God—alas we speak of it as if it were historically just once, and yet you do it constantly, many times every single day, throughout the whole of life, you always love us first. When we awake in the morning and turn our thoughts to you—you are the first, you have loved us first. If I were to rise at daybreak and instantly turn my thoughts to you in prayer, you are already there ahead of me. You have loved me first. When out of my distractions I collect my thoughts and think of you, you are there first ... always—and yet we talk ungratefully as if it were only once that you loved us first that way! [italics original] [25]

---

[24] See St. Bonaventure, *The Journey of the Mind to God*, VII, 1–2, trans. Philoteus Boehner, ed. Stephen F. Brown (Indianapolis: Hackett, 1956), pp. 37–38.

[25] Søren Kierkegaard, *Diary,* X3, 421, in *Kierkegaard's Journals and Notebooks*, vol. 7, gen. eds. Bruce H. Kirmmse and K. Brian Söderquist (Princeton, NJ: Princeton University Press, 2014), p. 478.

CHAPTER 3

"He has gone in to be the guest of a man who is a sinner"
JESUS AND ZACCHAEUS

1. Jesus and Sinners

We begin the second stage of our "exploration" of the river of mercy that flows through history, or better, we begin our second "plunge" into the pool of Bethsaida, which from this point on will be the Gospel. With the Incarnation, Jesus became "the visible face of the invisible God."[26] He told his apostles, "He who has seen me has seen the Father" (John 14:9). The God who is "merciful and gracious, slow to anger, and abounding in steadfast love and faithfulness" (Exodus 34:6) can only be contemplated now in the face of his Son made man. That is what we will do in the following chapters, meditating first on Christ's acts of mercy and then on his teaching about mercy.

Jesus encountered many people throughout the different areas of Palestine. The Gospels have transmitted a record of some of these people and given us their names for the most part. One prominent detail immediately leaps out at us: the women and men he meets are almost always in difficult situations or are suffering from

---

[26] See St. Irenaeus, *Against the Heresies*, IV, 6, 6, p. 392 (*"visibile Patris Filius"*).

a sickness, from grief, or from some other painful situation. Or worse, they are people living in moral situations in contradiction to the requirements of the Mosaic law and thus not according to God's will.

The preconceived notion of the future Messiah led people (including the apostles) to believe that Jesus would be brandishing lightning bolts of divine wrath. But instead, no! He deliberately aligned himself directly with the Father's love for his people, a love that was not commensurate with the merits of the people of Israel. The prophets, immediately after pronouncing threats because of the hardening of the people's hearts, presented themselves as heralds of this love that was never held back and never disavowed on God's part. Through the prophets and the psalms, God had already proclaimed that his love is freely given, that it cannot be bought and sold like merchandise. And yet, despite all this insistence, people ended up practicing a rigid and legalistic religion in which there was no place for mercy.

Mercy was precisely the extraordinary aspect about Jesus that fascinated the crowds of poor people, sinners of every kind, and those excluded from society and religion. Jesus jumbled up all the traditions. Sinners were people who were considered unclean because of their personal conduct or their disreputable professions, but he spent time with them. The murmurings that arose from the scribes and Pharisees about this were protests full of animosity. And from their vantage point, they had good reason!

The very word "Pharisee" indicated a separate, distinct category of people. They were "clean" and obliged to flee even minimal contact with sinners. Jesus, on the other hand, not only did not flee from these people but also seemed entirely at ease in their company and even sat at table with them. He did not place any conditions for them to approach him. In the eyes of the scribes and Pharisees, therefore, he could not be someone who had come from God because it is not possible for God to be compliant with or to approve of such disregard for his own laws!

This seems to have been the agonizing difficulty that drove his precursor, John the Baptist, to send a delegation of his disciples to Jesus to ask him in no uncertain terms, "Are you he who is to come, or shall we look for another?" (Matthew 11:3). John had announced the coming of one who would bring a sword and fire to the world, but instead he had to come to terms with someone who would "not break a bruised reed / or quench a smoldering wick" (12:20). John's bewilderment is understandable, and Jesus was not, in fact, surprised by it. Knowing John's question was asked in good faith, Jesus pointed to the signs that would identify him as the authentic Messiah announced by the prophets.

But who were the sinners? Whom did this word describe? In line with the widespread tendency today to clear the Pharisees of the Gospel completely and to attribute the negative picture of them to later distortions by the Gospel writers, someone has maintained that this word "sinners" meant "deliberate and unrepentant transgressors of the law."[27] In other words, they were the common criminals and lawbreakers of that time. If that were the case, Jesus' adversaries were quite correct to be scandalized and to consider him an irresponsible and socially dangerous person. It would be as if a priest today would frequently visit the Mafia, Mafia families, and criminals in general and repeatedly accept their dinner invitations under the pretext of talking to them about God.

However, this is not actually how things were. Above all, Jesus did not "frequent" the homes of publicans and sinners. He went only once to each of these houses, but on each occasion people ended up changed. The fact is that the Pharisees had their own view of the law—what was in conformity or contradiction to it—and they considered those who did not conform to their practices as reprobates. Jesus does not deny that sin and sinners exist; he does not, as we will see, justify Zacchaeus' fraudulent practices or the woman's adultery. The fact that he refers to such people as "those who are sick" (Matthew 9:12) demonstrates that.

What Jesus condemns is the Pharisees' claim, taking place then as it does today, that they are able to determine on their own what true righteousness is and, based on that criterion, to consider all others as "extortioners, unjust, adulterers" (Luke 18:11), denying even the possibility that such people could change. St. Paul, in speaking about the relentless defenders of the law, also notes that they often do exactly what they reprove others for doing (see

---

[27] See E. P. Sanders, *Jesus and Judaism* (Minneapolis: Fortress Press, 1985), p. 385.

Romans 2:17-24). The way Luke introduces the parable of the Pharisee and the tax collector is revealing: "He also told this parable to some who trusted in themselves that they were righteous and despised others" (Luke 18:9). Jesus was more critical of those who scornfully condemned sinners than of sinners themselves.[28]

2. "Zacchaeus, come down!"

Let us reflect on one of Jesus' encounters with sinners, the one in the home of Zacchaeus that Luke narrates in chapter 19. There are two scenes and settings: one takes place outdoors, and the other inside the home. The first occurs in the midst of the crowd, the other just between Jesus and Zacchaeus.

Jesus arrives in Jericho. This is not the first time he has come here, and this time, as he approaches the city, he heals a blind man (see Luke 18:35ff), which explains why such a large crowd was waiting for him. Zacchaeus is "a chief tax collector, and rich" (19:2). Because he is short, he climbs a tree along the route of the procession to see Jesus better. (At the entrance to Jericho, people still point out an old sycamore today that could have been Zacchaeus' sycamore!) And here is what happens: "And when Jesus came to the place, he looked up and said to him, 'Zacchaeus, make haste and come down; for I must stay at your house today.' So he made haste and came down, and received him joyfully. And

---

[28] See J. D. G. Dunn, *Christianity in the Making*, vol. 1, *Jesus Remembered* (Grand Rapids: Eerdmans, 2003), p. 532.

when they saw it they all murmured, 'He has gone in to be the guest of a man who is a sinner'" (19:5-7).

The citizens despised Zacchaeus because he was compromised by money and power and perhaps scorned him because he was short. Zacchaeus is nothing but a "sinner" to them. Jesus, on the other hand, goes to his house; he leaves the crowd of admirers that welcomed him to Jericho and visits only Zacchaeus. He is acting like the good shepherd who leaves the ninety-nine sheep to go find the hundredth sheep that is lost. For Jesus, Zacchaeus is above all "a son of Abraham" (Luke 19:9).

On the Sunday when this passage of the Gospel is read (the Thirty-first Sunday in Ordinary Time, Cycle C), the passage that gets read right before it—as a key to the Gospel reading—is about God's compassion:

> But thou art merciful to all, for thou canst do all things,
> and thou dost overlook men's sins, that they may repent.
> For thou lovest all things that exist,
> and hast loathing for none of the things which thou hast made.
> (Wisdom 11:23-24)

Jesus is acting, then, in the same manner as God. He welcomes those who are either outcasts of the political system (the poor and oppressed) or who are rejected by the religious system (pagans, tax collectors, and prostitutes). People who do not accept this kind of action by God exclude themselves from salvation; in wanting to discriminate at all costs, they end up being discriminated against. Seen in this light, the Zacchaeus episode seems like the parable of the tax collector and the Pharisee actually coming to pass: in the parable, God justified the repentant tax collector and sent the Pharisee away empty-handed. In this case, Jesus brings salvation to Zacchaeus' house and leaves the arrogant, sanctimonious people murmuring outside.

Let us go inside the house with Jesus and Zacchaeus and hear the rest of the story: "And Zacchaeus stood and said to the Lord, 'Behold, Lord, the half of my goods I give to the poor; and if I have defrauded any one of anything, I restore it fourfold.' And Jesus said to him, 'Today salvation has come to this house, since he also is a son of Abraham. For the Son of man came to seek and to save the lost'" (Luke 19:8-10).

3. Mercy (Not Reproach) Brings about the Miracle

Let us stop to reflect a bit more deeply on this episode. There were several reasons tax collectors were despised by the people. They were well-to-do and unscrupulous, which explains the hate and envy of the people who were burdened by taxes.

Zacchaeus, a chief tax collector, heard Jesus talked about as a prophet who is different from the others, so he wants to see him. There is certainly something more than sheer curiosity on Zacchaeus' part. He has a real interest, even though it is too early to consider a desire on his part to convert. Since Zacchaeus is short, he cannot see much, so he climbs up a tree. Jesus arrives and looks up—from many hints in the Gospels, it seems that Jesus' eyes had a miraculous power and spoke more than his words—and he calls Zacchaeus by name.

We might expect that before proclaiming forgiveness for him, he would require the five conditions that are normally demanded to obtain the remission of sin: examination of conscience, repentance, a firm resolve not to sin again, a confession of sin, and penance. But none of that happens! Jesus says, "Zacchaeus, make haste and come down; for I must stay at your house today" (Luke 19:5). The issue here is urgent: it has to happen now. He wants to spend time with Zacchaeus and not just go by his house to see where he lives. He wants to enter Zacchaeus' home, stay for a while, have a meal there, and perhaps spend the night.

Jesus compromises himself openly and dangerously because he risks becoming unclean himself. We know about Peter's resistance to entering the house of Cornelius the centurion to avoid becoming contaminated (see Acts of the Apostles 10). It is a natural reaction because such a thing could cause scandal. Jesus meets with a sinner at his home and does not impose any preliminary conditions on him. He does not ask him to purify himself, to "get himself sorted out" in terms of the Mosaic law; he does not ask him to leave his disreputable profession or to do restitution or penance.

Zacchaeus, however, is able to read in Jesus' gaze the same love that Jesus elsewhere directed to the rich young man (see Mark 10:21), and that gaze affects him. It is more than enough to fill

Zacchaeus with extraordinary joy. He welcomes this presence that lavishes him with unconditional love; he lets himself be swept away by this love. And it is precisely due to this love that he feels himself come back to life and become a human being again. He no longer feels the cloud of disdain over himself that had always accompanied him, even when he was dealing with his colleagues and subordinates.

Zacchaeus immediately understood that if he wanted this love to be alive and life-giving for him, he needed to let all of his life be inundated by it; he needed to allow it to influence all his relationships with other human beings. And so, spontaneously, without Jesus asking anything of him, Zacchaeus announces that he will give half of his goods to the poor and will restore fourfold to anyone from whom he collected more taxes than were owed.

It is, of course, true that a reparation is occurring here, but it is a reparation that takes place on the level of human relationships, in the sphere of justice operating among human beings. And it is in this sphere that his reparation deserves respect. However, Zacchaeus does not do this because of a condition imposed on him by Jesus in order to receive his love. It is instead a consequence of that love. Having been loved first, and freely, Zacchaeus feels the urge to turn toward others, toward those he has defrauded up to that time, and he learns to respect and love them. This is how God's mercy operates. Let us never forget it.

Chapter 4

"Neither do I condemn you"
Jesus and the Woman Caught in Adultery

1. Jesus and the Accusers

The episode of the woman caught in adultery is a mini-drama with two acts or scenes. The first scene includes many people: the accusers, the woman, and Jesus. The second scene has only two people, Jesus and the woman. Let us read what is reported about the first scene:

> Early in the morning he came again to the temple; all the people came to him, and he sat down and taught them. The scribes and the Pharisees brought a woman who had been caught in adultery, and placing her in the midst they said to him, "Teacher, this woman has been caught in the act of adultery. Now in the law Moses commanded us to stone such. What do you say about her?" This they said to test him, that they might have some charge to bring against him. Jesus bent down and wrote with his finger on the ground. And as they continued to ask him, he stood up and said to them, "Let him who is without sin among you be the first to throw a stone at her." And once more he bent down and wrote with his finger on the ground. But when they

heard it, they went away, one by one, beginning with the eldest, and Jesus was left alone with the woman standing before him. (John 8:2-9)

Let us reconstruct the scene mentally. Jesus is teaching in the Temple. Suddenly the circle of listeners opens up for a woman being pushed forward by a group of noisy Pharisees. They bring her to the front and form a circle around her, probably with their arms locked together. They say that the woman was "caught" in adultery, but one suspects the woman was not exactly "caught" (the scene takes place "early in the morning"); she has probably been spied on during different nights to make sure they have a case. Removed by force from the arms of her lover, the woman is taken to Jesus.

"What do you say about her?" They have not come to ask his opinion but to lay a trap for him, just like the time they had asked him if it was permissible to pay tribute to Caesar (see Matthew 22:17-21). The trap here is that if he says not to stone her, he is opposing the Law of Moses; he could be accused of being a transgressor because not only is adultery prohibited in the Decalogue, but the punishment of death by stoning for this sin is also explicitly stated there. If, on the other hand, Jesus says to stone her, he would in the end lose his reputation as a good teacher who is merciful to sinners and who attracts the favor of the people. They have devised the whole trap very well and are sure of being victorious.

Jesus reacts in a surprising way. He remains silent, bends down, and begins to write on the ground. He probably did not trace just signs, like some say, but letters. Some people think he was writing down the sins of the accusers, or he did this to show his indifference to the scribes and Pharisees. But Jesus never demonstrates indifference, let alone disdain toward others, no matter who they are.

Because the adultery is a duly attested flagrant crime, the man involved should have been taken to Jesus along with the woman. It is written in the law, "If a man commits adultery with the wife of his neighbor, both the adulterer and the adulteress shall be put to death" (Leviticus 20:10). Why didn't the scribes and Pharisees do this? Their assertion that the Law of Moses commanded them to stone this woman, while overlooking the man involved, is a distortion of the law that is just as blatant. Jesus does not want to humiliate his opponents too much in front of the people in noting that they themselves are in default with regard to the law. He prefers to observe that they would do better to examine themselves, so he bends down to write the sections of the law about the crime of adultery on the ground.

At first the scribes and Pharisees do not understand. Then Jesus lifts up his head and indicates a track they could take: "Let him who is without sin among you be the first to throw a stone at her." Their eyes are finally opened, and they read what he has written on the ground. Those who have more familiarity with the law, the oldest ones, are the first to understand his words. They do not need to stay any longer because they know the rest of the citations.

Nothing is left except for them to leave on tiptoes because they have been caught in their own trap.

Jesus wants them to understand, with tactfulness but firmness, that if human beings place themselves on the apparently solid ground of the law and the most approved and accepted morality in order to denounce the errors of others, they risk very soon having placed before them—like a mirror—the same law and the same morality, which now backfires on them! Who can presume to be righteous before God?

2. Jesus and the Woman, Alone

Let us move on to the second scene, which takes place just between Jesus and the woman. "Jesus was left alone with the woman standing before him. Jesus looked up and said to her, 'Woman, where are they? Has no one condemned you?' She said, 'No one, Lord.' And Jesus said, 'Neither do I condemn you; go, and do not sin again'" (John 8:9-11).

The tribunal is empty; only the judge and the accused remain. Up until this point, Jesus has remained bent down over the ground. Now he gets up, looks at the woman, and says, "Woman, where are they? Has no one condemned you?" The title "woman" on Jesus' lips does not sound scornful the way it did on the lips of the accusers ("this woman . . . such [a woman]"); it now sounds respectful and as if he is honoring her. It is the same title he uses to address his mother from the height of the cross: "Woman, behold, your son!" (John 19:26).

In the silence following the departure of her accusers, who knows with what trembling voice the woman answers Jesus, "No one, Lord." And Jesus says, "Neither do I condemn you; go, and do not sin again." This is an unprecedented statement when we think that Jesus had shown himself to be more severe than Moses in regard to adultery: "But I say to you that every one who looks at a woman lustfully has already committed adultery with her in his heart" (Matthew 5:28).

Being the only one without sin, Jesus could have, strictly speaking, thrown the first stone. But he does not do that; he does not condemn her, he cannot condemn her. In her look he understands that this woman has not yet been able to have an authentic human life, one that is willed by God. She has not yet been truly loved for herself. Things must not have been going well with her husband because she has a lover. Does this other man love her for herself or for his own sake? In the hands of the scribes and Pharisees, then, this woman is nothing but an object, a "pretext" to accuse Jesus. Not being loved for herself, how could this woman ever grasp the truth about loving others and the kind of love God requires between a man and woman? This is a concrete illustration of what human beings have become because of sin: they crave one another, they use one another to their own advantage, almost as if they were objects.

Jesus came especially to redeem human beings from this situation, to manifest to them how much they are loved for themselves, freely, without any preconditions. This is why Jesus cannot condemn the woman. He needs above all to reveal to her that he does not love her the way the others have, that is, to possess her, to use her like property. He makes a gift of love wholly directed toward her; he wants her finally to recover her dignity as a woman and as a full-fledged human being, the way the Father has wanted for her. Only after she discovers the blossoming of this love will the woman find—in this fountain now flowing in her innermost being—the capacity to love others for themselves the way she is loved.

The statement Jesus addresses to her—"Go, and do not sin again"—is not a threat. It is an invitation, although an urgent one, of course, because it allows for the freely given love lavished on her by the Father to permeate her whole existence and her relationships with others. From the moment that she knows she is loved, and loved this way, the woman should now learn to love in light and in truth herself. If Jesus had only taught her a "lesson in morals," this woman would not have been able to find life. This difference is still what is in play today concerning the efficacy or the failure of the Church's preaching.

Will the woman succeed in radically changing her life and stop sinning? That is possible, but we are not told! God respects everyone's freedom. After having met him, after having recognized and accepted his freely given love, this woman could sin again. And so the exhortation "Go, and do not sin again" can take on a tone that tends to sound like a threat for people who run the risk of losing their souls. However, we have to remember what Jesus said to Peter: "I do not say to you seven times, but seventy times seven" (Matthew 18:22). We need to go as far as we can with forgiveness because hatred has gone much farther. Needing to forgive "seventy times seven" indicates the fullness of forgiveness that is required. In other words, we never need to condemn and we always need to forgive, without putting limits on mercy based either on a timeframe or on people's intentions.

3. No to Sin, Yes to the Sinner

Her terror now behind her, the woman experiences Jesus' gaze of mercy as balm that flows into her heart. No man has ever looked at her that way! What new confidence Jesus' "Go" must have instilled in the woman! At that moment it meant, "Go back to living, to hoping; go back home; return to your dignity as a woman; announce to the men, just through your presence among them, that there is not only the law, there is also grace; there is not only justice, there is also mercy."

To understand what the woman experiences, we need to think of a woman condemned to death who is suddenly told by a friend that she has received a reprieve. Up until a minute before, the adulteress was about to be condemned to death and immediately executed, but now she is free. However, there is more: in her case, it is not just the expected punishment that is lifted, but also the sin that is canceled. She is free, not only outside in the sight of other people, but also inside before God. She is justified like the publican when he leaves the Temple.

This passage in the Gospel has always disturbed Christians a bit. It has only recently been inserted into the Sunday liturgy. We can understand the difficulty of admitting this passage into the canon of Scripture and why many ancient codices omit it. At a time when adultery was considered a sin with no possibility of forgiveness by the Church, Jesus' approach, which does not involve even a healthy penance for adultery, could only be disconcerting. There was more reason to remove this passage if it was found in some Gospel manuscripts than to add it if it was missing in some of them. However, there is no serious reason to doubt the historicity of the event, even if it was not John who wrote the account.

In the episode of the adulteress, Jesus does not disown the Mosaic law; he only reveals the provisional and contingent character of some of its prescriptions, in this case the sentence of stoning. In regard to an analogous disposition against women—the bill of divorce—Jesus says, "For your hardness of heart Moses allowed you to divorce your wives, but from the beginning it was not so" (Matthew 19:8). In this case as well, then, Jesus does not come to abolish the law but to perfect it and bring it to its completion.

Jesus does not say that adultery is not a sin or is just a small matter. There is an explicit condemnation of it, even if it is very delicately put, in the words "Do not sin again." Adultery remains a devastating sin that no one can comfortably keep on his or her conscience for long without damaging—besides the family—his or her own soul. It puts people in a state of living in "non-truth," forcing them constantly to dissimulate and lead a double life full of lies and subterfuge. It hardens one's heart to the point of trying to blame the situation in every possible way on the other spouse—always, in any case, to blame others. Adultery is not only a betrayal of a spouse but also of oneself. Jesus does not intend to approve what the woman has done in any way; what he is focused on condemning here is the attitude of people who are always ready to discover and denounce the sins of others.

But we need to be careful because here we risk becoming those who throw the first stone! We condemn the Pharisees in the Gospels because they are without mercy for their neighbor's misdeeds, and we are perhaps not aware that we often do exactly the same thing. We no longer throw stones at whoever does wrong (civil law would forbid that!), but we do throw mud and hurl slander and criticism at them. If someone in our circle of acquaintances falls or is gossiped about, we are suddenly scandalized about that person just like the Pharisees were. Often it is not because we really detest the sin that was committed but because we despise the sinner. This Gospel section on the adulteress proposes a great remedy for this bad habit. Let us examine ourselves well from God's vantage point, and then we will indeed feel the need to run to Jesus—but to ask pardon for ourselves and not to ask for the condemnation of others.

Chapter 5

"I desire mercy, and not sacrifice"
The Conversion of Matthew

1. Matthew Got Up and Followed Him

There is something moving in the call of Matthew the tax collector (see Matthew 9:9-13). The story of his life-changing encounter with Christ is an autobiographical account: "As Jesus passed on from there, he saw a man called Matthew sitting at the tax office; and he said to him, 'Follow me.' And he rose and followed him" (9:9).

Caravaggio has left us a famous painting depicting this scene. The future apostle is seated at a table. In addition to the money on the table, there is a pen and an inkwell. (They will serve one day for another purpose!) Light is coming from Christ's face and follows the movement of his hand, illuminating the faces of Matthew and the others seated with him at the tax table. It is a suggestive way of saying that the actual calling is accompanied by inner light. Without that suggestion, in fact, there is no rationale for the readiness with which Matthew gets up, leaves everything behind, and follows Christ without any need for explanation. The invisible dialogue between Christ and the future apostle is captured in their hand gestures. The hand of Christ, who is standing up, is extended in Matthew's direction as a sign of election more than of command. (There is no finger pointing to Matthew, just an out-stretched hand!) In response to that gesture, Matthew has his hand on his breast, like someone who is astonished at the choice and is asking, "Me? Are you sure you want me?"

Jesus, in the face of the refusal of the rich young man to follow him, had sadly observed, "It is easier for a camel to go through the eye of a needle than for a rich man to enter the kingdom of God" (Matthew 19:24). When the apostles then asked, "'Who then can be saved?'" Jesus answered, "With men this is impossible, but with God all things are possible" (19:25, 26). The call of Matthew is the confirmation that it is possible for God to save even a rich man. A comparison between the reaction of the rich young man to Jesus' invitation and Matthew's reaction also tells us something about him, about his openness to God. It was not at all predictable that Matthew would respond with such swiftness to Jesus' proposition. The rich young man, after Jesus' invitation, "went away sorrowful" (19:22), but Matthew "rose and followed him" (9:9).

Matthew's behavior seems at first somewhat implausible. We can imagine him seated, focused on collecting tolls and greedily contemplating his portion of the money the merchants were depositing on the table. He is in high spirits, but everything that has given meaning to his life up to that moment now loses its value. Matthew gets up, leaves everything, and follows Jesus. He has not witnessed any miracles, since this is almost at the beginning of Jesus' public ministry and Jesus is not yet famous. So how do we explain such readiness? Caravaggio has captured the answer on his canvas: the gaze of Jesus! Translations say that Jesus "saw a man," but perhaps it would be better to translate it as "he gazed at a man." Venerable Bede says that Jesus looks upon Matthew with "a gaze of mercy and election,"[29] "*miserando atque eligendo*"—"having mercy and choosing"—the words that Pope Francis has chosen as the motto for his papal coat of arms.[30]

2. "I came not to call the righteous, but sinners"

The episode of Matthew's call is not recorded chiefly because of the personal importance it had for him as the author of this Gospel, since both Mark and Luke refer to it, calling Matthew by his second name, Levi (see Mark 2:14; Luke 5:27). The interest is due to the statement that Jesus makes during the meal offered by Matthew in his house before taking leave of his former colleagues who were "tax collectors and sinners" (Matthew 9:10). As often happens, a Gospel episode is handed down thanks to a *logion*, a saying, of Jesus that is tied to it, and the event serves as a framework for the saying. Jesus responds to the scandalized reaction of the Pharisees at his entering the house of a tax collector and eating with sinners by saying, "Those who are well have no need of a physician, but those who are sick. Go and learn what this means, 'I desire mercy, and not sacrifice.' For I came not to call the righteous, but sinners" (Matthew 9:12-13).

---

[29] See Venerable Bede, "Homily 22," *CCL*, 122, 149–151.
[30] See *Misericordiae vultus*, n. 8.

We are so inured to the words of the Gospel that we take them for granted and find them natural even when they are objectively "scandalous" and should at least raise questions. Does God prefer sinners to the righteous? Then what is the point of the law and the commandments? Such unsettling questions at times lead us to discover clarifying answers in the Gospel.

The explanation of Jesus' assertion is simple. Jesus did not come to *call* the righteous (as though righteous people existed before he came) but to *make* people righteous. The apostle says in the Letter to the Romans, "There is no distinction; since all have sinned and fall short of the glory of God, they are justified by his grace as a gift, through the redemption which is in Christ Jesus, whom God put forward as an expiation by his blood, to be received by faith" (Romans 3:22-25).

Jesus is not denying that a certain kind of righteousness existed before he came, a righteousness that comes from observing the law (see Philippians 3:6). He freely recognizes that kind of righteousness in the Pharisees, whom he continues to call "the righteous" without being ironic. He is merely trying to explain to them that this righteousness is not enough to save them because it cannot give life. It was only supposed to make people "long for grace" and help them recognize the moment of its coming. Having failed in its goal, their righteousness is now transformed into pseudo-righteousness, an inadequate righteousness that cannot save. This was the dramatic situation of Christ's opponents; the apostle says of them mournfully that "being ignorant of the righteousness that comes from God, . . . [they sought] to establish their own" (Romans 10:3).

We see all this already played out in Matthew's life. The encounter with Christ has made him "justified"; he was "a publican and a sinner," but being made righteous has now made him a new person, an apostle of Christ. If Matthew had remained a tax collector, Caravaggio's choice to paint him (to mention but the least of Matthew's glories) would not have occurred, and the world would not have even known there existed a certain Matthew called Levi.

3. Mercy and Sacrifice

There remains an obscure point to clarify. In light of what has been said, what does the statement from Hosea 6:6 that Christ repeats—"I desire mercy, and not sacrifice"—really mean? Is every sacrifice and mortification then pointless, and is loving really enough by itself to set a person right with God? Countless people interpret it this way and teach that to others. This passage could make people end up rejecting the whole ascetic aspect of Christianity as a residue of a troubling or Manichean mentality that has since been overcome.

Once again an unsettling question becomes an opportunity for an enlightening discovery. First and foremost, a profound change of perspective occurs when the statement passes from Hosea to Christ. In Hosea the statement refers to people and to what God wants from them. God wants love and knowledge of himself from people, not their sacrifices and burnt offerings. However, on Jesus' lips, the saying refers instead to God. The love he is talking about is not the love that God requires of people but the love he gives to human beings. "I desire mercy, and not sacrifice" (Matthew 9:13; 12:7) means, "I want to apply mercy, not condemnation." The biblical equivalent of this concept is the verse we read in Ezekiel: "I have no pleasure in the death of the wicked, but that the wicked turn from his way and live" (33:11). God does not want to "sacrifice" human beings but to save them.

With this qualification, we understand Hosea's saying better as well. God does not want sacrifice "at all costs," as if he delights in seeing us suffer. He does not want sacrifice so that people can stake their claims and declare their merits before him, nor does he want sacrifice out of a misunderstood sense of duty. He does, however, desire the sacrifice that is required by his love and by the observance of his commandments. "There is no living of love without sorrow," says *The Imitation of Christ* (III, 5), and our daily experience confirms that. There is no love without sacrifice. It is in this sense that Paul exhorts us to make our whole lives "a living sacrifice, holy and acceptable to God" (Romans 12:1).

Sacrifice and mercy are both good things, but they can each become something unhealthy if misdirected. They are good things if one chooses sacrifice for oneself and mercy for others, the way Christ did. However, both become unhealthy if we do the opposite and choose mercy for ourselves but sacrifice for others, if we are lenient with ourselves but strict with others, always ready to excuse ourselves and merciless in judging others. Do we really not have something to examine about our conduct in this respect?

We cannot conclude these comments on Matthew's call without turning our thoughts affectionately and gratefully to this Evangelist who often accompanies us during the course of the liturgical year with his Gospel. We do that with some verses about Matthew by Paul Claudel. (The poet knows the traditional symbol for Matthew is an angel but says elsewhere that he prefers the symbol of the ox for him.)

And Matthew, the publican, who first had the idea,
Knowing the power of a written text, of setting down
   in black on a page
Jesus—exactly what he had said and what their eyes had seen.
In doing this, taking up the instrument he had once
   used to do calculations,
Conscientious, calm, imperturbable as an ox,
He began to plow his great field of white paper.
He plows a furrow, he turns to begin another so that
   nothing will be omitted
Of what his memory offers and of what the Holy Spirit
   dictates to him.
Not just for his age, but for the whole Church that will come. [31]

---

[31] Paul Claudel, *Corona benignitatis anni Dei, Saint Matthieu* (Paris: Gallimard, 1967), p. 421; see also his play, *The Satin Slipper* [*Le soulier de satin*], Day IV, scene 6.

CHAPTER 6

A Woman with a Flask of Ointment
JESUS AND THE SINFUL WOMAN

There are some passages in the Gospel in which the teaching is so tied to the action that the teaching cannot be fully understood if it is detached from the action. The episode of the sinful woman in Simon's house is one such instance. We cannot in this case identify the central message and then follow the action. Just the opposite is true here: we need to follow the developing action to end up finally being able to extract the message.

It is a very colorful passage with at least four changes of perspective in the story corresponding to the different people in the situation: the woman, the Pharisee, Jesus, and the dinner guests. Let us leave aside what this last group says ("Who is this, who even forgives sins?" [Luke 7:49]) because it touches on a theme that we will focus on later. Let us just focus on the first three protagonists.

1. Jesus and the Woman

The first scene is silent; there are no words, just silent actions:

> One of the Pharisees asked him to eat with him, and he went into
> the Pharisee's house, and sat at table. And behold, a woman of
> the city, who was a sinner, when she learned that he was sitting at

table in the Pharisee's house, brought an alabaster flask of ointment, and standing behind him at his feet, weeping, she began
to wet his feet with her tears, and wiped them with the hair of
her head, and kissed his feet, and anointed them with the ointment. (Luke 7:36-38)

Defying all taboos, the woman approaches Jesus and kneels at
his feet. The scene is surprising, and at first glance it can only be
scandalous. This woman is, in fact, known by everyone to be a sinner. She is probably not a prostitute by trade but a woman of easy
virtue, a loose woman. She is a woman who knows how to behave
with men. Her actions give the scene a very sensual atmosphere. It
is enough to trouble a normal man: tears, long hair, kisses, caresses,
perfume! But Jesus does not move and just lets her do it!

We could imagine that she has already seen him and heard him
and has been deeply touched by him. She must have sought information about his whereabouts because she knows just where to
find him. She has sensed that through this man she can regain the
purity and truth she has lost in her life. She feels that he will not
condemn her or scorn her or use her as an object. So she comes to
him and confusedly tries to express this whole combination of sentiments. But she only knows how to act in this ambiguous manner.
To demonstrate her desire to be forgiven, this woman only knows
how to offer what she has offered other men. She also does what
the Pharisee should have done but did not do: she washes his feet
and anoints them with perfume.

Jesus accepts all this because pushing her away would have been like consigning her to her "non-life." By letting her be, he lets her know, infinitely better than long speeches would have, that he accepts what she is able to offer him because he loved her even before she presented herself at his feet. And he loves her without trying to take the least little thing from her for himself. He accepts her just as she is simply because she needs to know, first and foremost, that she is loved and finally respected. He does not judge or condemn her. He brings her back to life, to an authentically human life.

At this point, the woman understands that this man will turn her life upside down. She is no longer taking the first step to attract men to give them pleasure. It is Christ who first makes a gift of love, which she now realizes she had never received before. The kind of love she has been experiencing was a caricature of love. In Jesus' presence this woman is like an impoverished creature who realizes she must first receive everything from him if she truly wants to give all afterwards.

2. Jesus and the Pharisee

The focus now shifts to the Pharisee who has invited Jesus to dinner. The scene is still silent, but only outwardly, since the Pharisee speaks to himself: "Now when the Pharisee who had invited him saw it, he said to himself, 'If this man were a prophet, he would have known who and what sort of woman this is who is touching him, for she is a sinner'" (Luke 7:39).

On the surface, the Pharisee seems kind in trying to excuse Jesus, attributing Jesus' acceptance of what she is doing to ignorance: "Poor guy, he doesn't know who's touching him!" But he does this at the price of a much more serious accusation: "Jesus is not a prophet, let alone the prophet we have been waiting for in these last days; he is usurping the fame he enjoys since he is deceiving himself as well as the people."

At this point in the Gospel text, and only at this point, does Jesus speak to give his opinion about the woman's actions and the Pharisee's thinking:

> And Jesus answering said to him, "Simon, I have something to say to you." And he answered, "What is it, Teacher?" "A certain creditor had two debtors; one owed five hundred denarii, and the other fifty. When they could not pay, he forgave them both. Now which of them will love him more?" Simon answered, "The one, I suppose, to whom he forgave more." And he said to him, "You have judged rightly." (Luke 7:40-43)

Jesus first gives his host the chance to be persuaded that he is, in fact, a prophet, given that he can read the thoughts of his heart. At the same time, through the parable he is preparing the people there to understand what he is saying in defense of the woman who, by washing his feet, kissing them, and pouring perfume on them, has done for him what the master of the house did not do. "'Therefore I tell you, her sins, which are many, are forgiven, for she loved much; but he who is forgiven little, loves little.' And he said to her, 'Your sins are forgiven'" (Luke 7:47-48).

A certain divergence has been remarked upon between the parable told by Jesus and its application to the case of the woman. According to the parable, *forgiveness is the cause of love*: the woman loves much because she has been forgiven much. In the application, *love is the cause of forgiveness*: she is forgiven many sins because she loved much. In the first case, God takes the initiative, and in the second, it seems to be the woman who takes the initiative. There is no need for recourse to some kind of acrobatics to resolve the difficulty here. In spiritual things there is always a kind of circularity and reciprocity. God's forgiveness creates grateful love in a person, and after a person makes a humble confession of sin, his or her love is perfected and increases. Both things can therefore be true.

3. Jesus and Us

The Gospel account ends here. What can be expected from whoever reads this account? It is clear that, according to Luke's intention in reporting it, the episode of the sinful woman should make us understand the spirit of Christ and his message of salvation for the poor, the sinners, the outcasts. Luke was not writing his Gospel for the Pharisees but for Christians, and particularly for Christians coming out of paganism. This means he considered Christ's lesson to be addressed not just to the Pharisees of a certain time period, but to everyone who would read this Gospel, including us.

The issue here is very relevant. It is a question of knowing what authentic spirituality consists in, what the most correct feeling or attitude before God is, what God values above all in human beings. According to a certain way of thinking, all of these questions are resolved by observing the law, understood, moreover, in a reductive way. The Pharisees focus all their attention on the precepts violated by publicans and prostitutes, while they gloss over other precepts, like that of love of neighbor, even though it is the clearest precept in the law.

This legalistic criterion leads to a division of people into two very clear categories: the righteous and sinners. There is, in fact, no room for the mercy that is God's most defining attribute because sinners do not deserve it and the righteous do not need it. This leads to the highly erroneous belief (the Pelagian heresy) that it is sufficient for God to reveal his will and give people his commandments because they are able to perform them through their will alone without needing anything else.

The woman silently shows us an altogether different religious universe that consists in the humble acknowledgment of sin, of a desire to change, and of gratitude to God who always gives human beings new possibilities for redemption, who wants mercy more than sacrifice, and who values love from a contrite heart more than any burnt offerings and sacrifices. In this scenario, human beings do not see themselves as God's creditors but always as debtors for everything.

The truest and most relevant goal of this section of the Gospel is realized when a person, man or woman, identifies naturally with the sinful woman. They recognize themselves fully in her and desire to repeat that woman's inner experience in their own lives. A genuine conversion took place in the woman's heart. For her to turn from a sinful life in the public square that was dominated by so many other preoccupations and thoughts to such different sentiments—who knows what kind of revolution took place in her heart? And all of it happened because she saw the man from Nazareth and listened to his words, perhaps at a distance. Through her actions, she was crying out only one thing to Christ: "I need you." And then he could respond to her, "Your faith has saved you; go in peace" (Luke 7:50). This is Jesus' style.

The conversion of the female protagonist in this Gospel episode seems to be the prototype for all the great conversions occasioned by an encounter with Christ: for example, the conversion of Paul, who now considers as "loss" and "refuse" what he had considered up to that time "gain" in his life (see Philippians 3:8); the conversion of Francis of Assisi, for whom "that which seemed bitter to me was changed into sweetness of soul and body," as he would say in his *Testament*.[32]

---

[32] St. Francis of Assisi, *The Testament*, in *Frances and Clare: The Complete Works*, trans. and intro. Regis J. Armstrong and Ignatius C. Brady (New York: Paulist Press, 1982), p. 154.

It is not expected that this should happen only once in our lives at the moment of our first conversion. Going from having a heart of stone to a heart of flesh does not happen only once. We often discover as life goes on that we have become distant from God with a heart that has hardened again and is in need of reconciliation with him and with ourselves. That is the time to remember this passage in the Gospel and listen to the voice of the Spirit who invites us to relive it.

If people seek to encounter Jesus today in order to have the experience of the sinful woman, they do not need to go far or to retreat into fantasy. Every day Jesus, who "sits at table with his disciples" (see Luke 22:30), can be found in the Eucharist. One can kneel at his feet, express repentance and gratitude, and each time experience the "joy and gladness" of being saved (see Psalm 51:8).

CHAPTER 7

*Mercy for People in
"Irregular" Situations*
JESUS AND THE SAMARITAN WOMAN

1. An Encounter outside the Norm

Returning from Jerusalem to Galilee on one occasion, Jesus was
going through Samaria. And in this region he had an encounter
at the well in Sychar with a Samaritan woman who is described
by John in an unusually detailed way (see John 4:5-42). The apostles had gone into the city to get some food; Jesus, weary from
his journey, had stopped at Jacob's well when a woman arrived
to draw water.

A respectable man would never speak to a woman he did not
know in a public place, and this time there is an additional reason:
she is a Samaritan woman! It is easy to understand the woman's
astonishment when Jesus asks her for something to drink. However,
Jesus' encounters are always characterized by his approaching people who are somehow "polluted" physically, morally, or spiritually.
As if this were not enough, the ensuing dialogue reveals that this
Samaritan woman is in a marital situation that is contrary to the
law. After having had five husbands, she is now living with a man
she is not married to. It is beside the point to discuss if she was
the one who changed husbands five times (something not so easy

for women to do then) or if she had been left by five husbands. It is also unessential to try to find out if they were legitimately husbands or simply men she lived with as a concubine. The Gospel writer did not consider it important to clarify any of these things for us to understand the message, and we only have that source of information.

There was really every reason in the world to avoid an encounter with such a woman! Instead, the Son of God is the one who takes the first step toward her. He is the one who asks her for something, who makes himself the suppliant, thus encouraging the woman to enter into a dialogue with him. He speaks to her explicitly about her irregular conjugal situation, but he does not command her to leave the man she is living with, nor does he ask her to live chastely with the man. And she is the person to whom Jesus first reveals that he is the Messiah. He asks for absolutely nothing. He looks at her and finds her infinitely lovable because she is infinitely loved by his Father despite all her sin and her ritual uncleanness. The fact that the Father loves her is enough for him. His unconditional love moves him to reveal to this woman what seems to be the "messianic secret" throughout the Gospel that should be kept hidden for fear of misunderstandings. Nothing is unforgivable in his eyes; love always forgives. It is significant that the account of the Samaritan woman is found in the same Gospel of John that relates the episode of the adulteress.

2. A New Beginning

What can we learn from Jesus' behavior with the Samaritan woman with regard to the pastoral problem of divorced and remarried people and, in general, so-called irregular unions? (I am using the current term while awaiting a word that is more respectful.) One thing, above all, I believe: her turnaround is the effect of an encounter with Jesus, and not the precondition for it.

The encounter with Christ creates a new beginning in the life of the Samaritan woman. She will be judged not on the basis of what she had done before but on the basis of what she does afterward, which is why she is always remembered with gentle affection in the Christian tradition. Thanks to her, many people in Samaria acknowledged the Messiah; she was a "gospel preacher," a sister to Magdalene who first brought the news of the resurrection to the apostles.

Now it is true in the case of believers who are divorced and remarried that their encounter with Jesus already happened in Baptism, and so on the surface they are similar to the Samaritan woman after her encounter with Christ. But here is the problem: was that baptismal encounter really an encounter, a personal encounter? Have these people ever really known the love of Christ? We describe "nominal" Christians today as those who have received Baptism without ever becoming "real believers" through their own decision, but in fact we act (and the law acts!) as though they were real Christians who were provided with all the means of grace to overcome the obstacles encountered in a marriage.

However, even if at one time these people were "real" Christians, that is, convinced and practicing Christians, is it in line with the gospel to exclude the possibility of a real repentance for them according to the practices during the first centuries whereby people were readmitted to full communion with the Church? The way Jesus deals with the Samaritan woman and, as we have seen, with the sinful woman who clasped his feet—is it not at least equivalent to what he does in giving himself in the Eucharist? If the Eucharist is "his true body born of the Virgin Mary,"[33] then in both cases (the reality and the sacrament), are we not dealing with the same identical Jesus?

We can use the kindest and most encouraging words toward divorced and remarried people who desire to live a Christian life, but the reality does not change. To refuse them sacramental absolution and the Eucharist in every case, even when they are repentant and have resolved to follow a path of reintegration into the community, means saying to them that they are in a state of mortal sin, that is, objectively separated from God, with the consequences we are aware of if they should die in such a state. Given the present increasing trend in society, this would lead before long to having a Christian community that was formed, for the most part or

---

[33] Hymn "Ave verum" (XIV c.), *Liber Usualis Missae et Officii* (Rome: Tournai, 1914), p. 1561.

nearly so, of "dead" members, because the Eucharist is the sacrament of the living.

St. Paul recognizes the possibility of divorce and remarriage for people who become believers if a spouse refuses to follow the other person in that decision (see 1 Corinthians 7:15). This is the so-called Pauline privilege, or "privilege of the faith," recognized by the Code of Canon Law.[34] That exception does not apply to baptized divorced people in all its juridical requirements, but there is, nevertheless, an unmistakable analogy that can be made in so many cases of divorced Christians (even if not in all).

According to traditional canon law, at least in the past, simple conversion to the Catholic Church, even from another Christian confession, Protestant or otherwise, authorized people to obtain *ipso facto* the right to divorce and remarry. Should we not allow the same thing for a person who has had a true and profound conversion to Christ and then cannot live with the first spouse?

3. "Let a man examine himself"

One thing is clear: the situation of people in the Church who are divorced and remarried cannot be resolved only by the law and only by canon law. The cases are too numerous and too varied, and it is impossible to govern them with a single regulation. If the sacraments are "for the sake of the people" (*propter homines*, as they say in theology), then the law, too, should be "for

---

[34] See the Code of Canon Law, 1143–1147.

the sake of the people" and not against them. This is what the wise ancient saying intended to express by "*summum jus, summa injuria*" ("extreme justice is extreme injustice"). When the law is carried to its extreme, it can become its opposite and be unjust.

It is inevitable in this area to appeal to people's consciences. The Church, in the Second Vatican Council, recognized that the conscience has supreme jurisdiction to which all other jurisdictions have to yield, including the magisterium, because it involves the direct and unalienable right of every person before God.[35] The Church and the magisterium should "form" the conscience, proclaiming the requirements of the gospel and natural laws with respect and clarity, but they cannot replace it.

The apostle Paul gives some rules and sets forth the requirements for us to approach receiving the Body of the Lord, but then he concludes by saying, "Let a man examine himself, and so eat of the bread and drink of the cup. For any one who eats and drinks without discerning the body eats and drinks judgment upon himself" (1 Corinthians 11:28-29). We need to try to have people who desire to receive the Eucharist understand this. It is pointless to be admitted to Communion if it then becomes a condemnation before God.

This applies to everyone, not just to those who have problems concerning their marriages. People could have "all their ducks in a row"—the preceding marriage annulled, a new marriage in the

[35] See Second Vatican Council, *Dignitatis humanae* [*Declaration on Religious Freedom*], n. 2ff.

Church—and nevertheless receive Communion to their condemnation because they never really examined themselves and submitted themselves to the judgment of God and of conscience. They have never taken responsibility for their own part in the failure of the first marriage but put all the blame on the other spouse, even denigrating that spouse in every way in the eyes of others. They have never reflected on the suffering and the damage caused to the children in depriving them of their own father or mother. They have never said what David said after taking the wife of one of his soldiers: "Have mercy on me, O God, / according to thy steadfast love; /. . . my sin is ever before me. / . . . [I have] done that which is evil in thy sight" (Psalm 51:1, 3-4).

4. The Gospel Model

In all the cases discussed so far (Zacchaeus, the adulterous woman, Matthew, the sinful woman, the Samaritan woman), the example of Christ tells us one thing we must never forget. A real change of heart will take place only when, first and foremost, people discover that they are loved for themselves and are precious in the eyes of God who, in every case, will never cease loving them. Communicating this truth is the loftiest duty of the Church and is the best way to preach mercy. To be convinced of this, we only need to look once more at how Jesus behaved during his life. What model or law is more authoritative than his example?

Jesus goes toward sinners, toward individuals who find themselves in situations contrary to the law. And as we have seen, how does he act? Does he erect insurmountable barriers between himself and them? Does he place conditions on them, knowing that they will not be able to observe them? Does he discourage them with his intransigence? No! He asks them for something to drink, confides his most intimate secret to them, and sits at table with them. Only later does he reveal to them the requirements of love.

It is legitimate, then, to dream of a Church that becomes more explicitly and boldly evangelical again in the footsteps of Christ, without being afraid of being at the side of the poor and of sinners, without being afraid of not always being understood. We can think, in particular, of some wounded men and women who still bear their wounds from life and whose love has been derailed, men and women who are trying to "make a new life" for themselves. These people need to know that God is near, to be persuaded deep in their hearts that they should never despair because the heavenly Father never stops having confidence in them. If they, like Zacchaeus and the Samaritan woman, had been alongside a road Jesus was walking on, he would certainly have invited himself to their table too.

During the course of the spiritual exercises preached in the presence of John Paul II in the Jubilee Year 2000, the late Vietnamese Cardinal Francis Xavier Van Thuan, a heroic witness of faith who had lived in his country's communist prisons for thirteen years (many of those years in isolation and unimaginable conditions), shared these words that take on a particular significance as we hear them again during this Jubilee Year of Mercy: "I dream of a church that is the *Holy Door*, always open, embracing all, full of compassion; and that understands the pain and sufferings of humanity, protecting and consoling all people."[36]

---

[36] Francis Xavier Van Thuan, *Testimony of Hope*, trans. Julia Mary Darrenkamp and Anne Eileen Heffernan (Boston: Pauline Press, 2000), p. 38.

CHAPTER 8

Believing in the Mercy of God
PETER AND JUDAS, TWO ALMOST PARALLEL STORIES

1. Jesus Fixed His Gaze on Him

The most striking fact when we read the Passion according to Mark is the prominence given to Peter's betrayal (14:66-72). It is first announced by Jesus at the Last Supper: "Truly, I say to you, this very night, before the cock crows twice, you will deny me three times" (14:30). And then Mark describes all its humiliating development: "I neither know nor understand what you mean. . . . I do not know this man of whom you speak" (14:68, 71).

This emphasis is significant because Mark was like a secretary to Peter and wrote his Gospel by putting together reports and information that came from Peter. It is therefore Peter himself who divulged the story of his betrayal and did a kind of public confession about it. In the joy of the forgiveness he had experienced, Peter did not care about his good name and his reputation as head of the apostles. He wanted anyone who might later fall the way he did not to despair of forgiveness.

Let us pause a bit on the details of this episode, which was so painful for Peter but is so instructive for us. It helps us understand (and avoid) the dynamic that leads to betrayal. When the young doorkeeper girl approached Peter in the high priest's courtyard to look at him by the light of the fire, Peter became afraid. He had not yet recovered from the fear he experienced when his sword had proved useless in the garden. He had started following Jesus again at a distance and had entered the high priest's courtyard with a certain apprehension. A word to the doorkeeper from John had allowed Peter to enter the palace area and go warm himself near the brazier in the courtyard.

The young servant girl was concerned about the presence of this unknown person, and noticing his insecure attitude, her suspicions grew. We know what her question was and what Peter's answer was. Then Peter moved away from her by going toward the vestibule, but the servant caught up to him here too and asked the same question and got an even more frightened answer: "I do not know this man!" (Mark 14:71). Meanwhile, a cock had crowed, but Peter did not notice because he was too preoccupied with guarding his own safety. In order not to look suspicious, he joined the conversation of the group there, but he was recognized by his Galilean accent as the one who had drawn his sword, so he could find no way of escape except to deny things all over again even more insistently!

The inner workings that led to this sin are revealed in Peter's successive and increasingly insistent denials. He was progressively being pulled into an unfaithfulness that was always more definitive to the point of that betrayal he would have thought impossible at the time he had begun to follow the Master. He had hoped to sidestep the danger simply by denying that he knew Jesus, but this behavior only exposed him to even further denunciations by the people there. After having denied Jesus the first time, Peter ended up denying him more forcefully a second and third time. His first lie, his first disloyalty, in addition to not extricating him from his predicament, put him in a situation that was harder and harder to get out of. It is an impressive example of the tendency of sin to multiply and escalate, even if it is due only to weakness, when it is based on a lie.

The second crowing of the cock happened in time to prevent Peter from ultimately getting stuck in his false declarations. And he remembered Jesus' prophecy. Disturbed by that memory, he moved away from the group. Precisely at that moment, Jesus exits the room where he was being interrogated by Caiaphas; he follows the guards who lead him away in chains, but he turns his head toward his disciple.

Here we see all of Christ's infinite mercy toward his disciple. He did not limit himself to announcing a warning ahead of time—the second crowing—to help stop Peter on his slippery slope, but he intervenes personally with a loving gaze to reconquer the heart of the one who had denied him. His gaze makes Peter aware of the sin he has committed. Up until that moment, Peter had let himself be guided instinctively by fear, by a desire to escape the suspicions of the people around him. In his denials he was thinking only of himself and safeguarding his life. He was not clearly aware of his unfaithfulness because he was avoiding thinking about it, and he did not want to be fully conscious of the import of his conduct. But Jesus suddenly appears before him and brings him back to reality.

Luke is the one who emphasizes the detail about Jesus' gaze as the cause of the apostle's sudden weeping: "And the Lord turned and looked at Peter. And Peter remembered the word of the Lord. . . . And he went out and wept bitterly" (Luke 22:61, 62). Jesus' gaze uncovers Peter's sin and wakes him up from his lack of self-consciousness better than the cock's crowing does. Jesus' gaze is a gaze of kindness that offers forgiveness. There is no anger, no irritation in it; the only reproach, gentle and silent, is that of a wounded affection. Jesus' gaze of mercy obtains the result that a reproachful gaze would not have had.

2. No Sin Too Great for God's Mercy

To understand the story of Peter's denial fully, we need to read it in parallel with the story of Judas' betrayal. That betrayal was also preannounced by Christ in the upper room and then took place in the Garden of Olives. When Jesus passed by Peter, he "turned and looked at Peter," but he did even more with Judas: he let himself be kissed by him. However, the outcomes were very different. Peter "went out and wept bitterly" (Luke 22:62), but Judas went out and hanged himself.

We need to understand the crux of the difference between the stories of Peter and Judas: why do they end in such different ways? Peter had remorse for what he had done, but Judas was also remorseful, to the point of crying out, "I have sinned in betraying innocent blood!" (Matthew 27:4) and returning the thirty pieces of silver. Where is the difference, then? Only in one thing: Peter trusted in the mercy of God and Judas did not.

The Bible presents us with a whole gallery of parallel stories about sin that end in diametrically opposite ways. It does so to move us toward making the right choice. Cain killed Abel and David killed Uriah, the husband of the woman he wanted for himself. And yet Cain is abhorred and David is honored. The reason is always the same. Cain despaired; he thought his sin was too great to be forgiven (see Genesis 4:13). David, on the other hand, trusted in God's mercy: "Have mercy on me, O God, / according to thy steadfast love; / according to thy abundant mercy blot out my transgressions" (Psalm 51:1).

On Calvary the same kind of scenario takes place again. There are two thieves, both of whom have sinned equally and are criminals. One, however, curses and insults Jesus and dies in despair. The other cries out, "Jesus, remember me when you come in your kingly power," and immediately he hears Jesus answer him, "Truly, I say to you, today you will be with me in Paradise" (Luke 23:42, 43).

The lesson that comes from the parallel but opposite stories of Peter and Judas is that there is never a need to despair of mercy. To do so means to consider our sin to be greater than God's mercy and means limiting God's power. In the Old Testament, God had already said,

"Come now, let us reason together,
　　says the LORD:
though your sins are like scarlet,
　　they shall be as white as snow;
though they are red like crimson,
　　they shall become like wool." (Isaiah 1:18)

What will God not do, now that the blood of his Son, which "speaks more graciously than the blood of Abel" (Hebrews 12:24), is between people's sins and his forgiveness? Every doubt and every temptation to despair should disappear before a saying like this one from John: "By this we shall know that we are of the truth, and reassure our hearts before him whenever our hearts condemn us; for God is greater than our hearts, and he knows everything" (1 John 3:19-20). The disciple that Jesus loved exclaims, "We know and believe the love God has for us. God is love, and he who abides in love abides in God, and God abides in him" (1 John 4:16). We should proclaim this in the first person with equal forcefulness: "I have known and therefore I believe in God's mercy!"

3. Sins against the Holy Spirit?

According to the older catechism of the Catholic Church, there are only two sins that can render God's mercy ineffective, and they are both referred to there as sins against the Holy Spirit.[37] The first is to *presume* to save oneself "without help from on high." [38] (It would be better to say, "to presume to save oneself by one's own merits instead of by grace and faith!") The second is that "by *despair*, man ceases to hope for his salvation [italics original]."[39] Presumption and despair. Now let us broach the famous "sin against the Holy Spirit" that Jesus said cannot be forgiven and that has caused anguish in so many hearts. The context explains what that particular sin involves: "'Truly, I say to you, all sins will be forgiven the sons of men, and whatever blasphemies they utter; but whoever blasphemes against the Holy Spirit never has forgiveness, but is guilty of an eternal sin'—for they had said, 'He has an unclean spirit'" (Mark 3:28-30).

First and foremost, it is clear that this deals with a particular—and not a universal—assertion limited to a situation taking place during Jesus' earthly life. It is the sin of those who identify the One who came to free people from Satan with Satan himself, thus excluding themselves from salvation. By extension, this is the

---

[37] They are referred to in the new catechism as sins against hope.

[38] This is how the new *Catechism of the Catholic Church*, 2092, refers to this sin.

[39] Ibid., 2091.

sin of those who consistently refuse to acknowledge Jesus as the Savior of the world and who think there is no "salvation" or eternal life for human beings. When people persist in this conviction, it is clear that there cannot be remission of sin for the simple fact that they do not ask for it and do not want it. In other words, there is no sin God cannot and does not want to forgive except the sin of someone who does not seek or want forgiveness.

Let us conclude with a story that, if not true, is nevertheless instructive. One time a young child who had heard the story of Judas said, with the candor and wisdom of children, "Judas was wrong about the tree to hang himself on; he chose a fig tree." The astonished catechist asked him, "And what should he have chosen?" "He should have hung himself around Jesus' neck!" The child was right. If Judas had hung on Jesus' neck and asked for forgiveness, he would be honored today no less than St. Peter.

CHAPTER 9

There Will Be Joy in Heaven over One Sinner Who Repents
THE PARABLES OF MERCY

1. This Is How God Acts!

If the gospel means "good news," and more precisely good news for the poor and for sinners, then chapter 15 in Luke with its three parables—the lost sheep, the lost drachma, and the prodigal son—takes us to the very heart of the gospel. The specific occasion that gives great unity to this grouping as a whole is that Jesus is defending his actions toward sinners against the accusations of his enemies. The parables are addressed to the scribes and Pharisees who "murmured, saying, 'This man receives sinners and eats with them'" (Luke 15:2).

To achieve his goal, Jesus takes a strange path: he invents situations, parables, that seem very true and deal with daily life but that are in fact unreal and contrary to experience. A real shepherd does not leave ninety-nine sheep in the desert because on his return, he would surely have one restored sheep and ninety-nine sheep who had wandered off. The very poor woman (she had to be poor if her dowry was only ten drachmas) cannot really invite her friends to have a feast with her because a simple snack would cost not just one but all ten of her drachmas. A Palestinian father does not give his younger son, who is less than eighteen years old (and in fact is not yet married), his part of the inheritance and, in addition, give it to him in the form of immediately liquidated funds. The customs of the time dictated that at most, a father who was still alive might hand over some property that was coming to the sons but not liquidated funds.

Jesus is illustrating God's action through these three practical situations. An air of truth, of things that are experienced and felt every day, seems to emanate from the three parables. This is all so natural, isn't it? Jesus seems to be saying, "Don't all shepherds and fathers on earth act this way?" And we naively follow him, nodding in agreement, without realizing that this is not really true and that none of us would act this way. Jesus is showing himself to be a great poet here. Just as only poets can do, he succeeds in making wonderful things seem true to actual experience even if they are only imagined. We are reminded of the great fable writers who know how to make animals speak in a way that makes them seem human. The situations created by Jesus in the parables are thus true, but on the higher level of divine, not human, truth. We are pulled along by them, and we enjoy the dissimulation because it pleases us more than reality and makes us feel better. How nice it would be if things really were this way!

I said that Jesus is using three practical situations to illustrate God's way of relating to human beings. They give us an image of God "in human clothes." Jesus is saying this is how God acts! These are his reactions; this is his weakness! We need to take God as he is; we need to excuse God for his weakness because he finds joy in it. There is no need to ask people why they find joy in a thing because they would answer, "That's the way I'm made!" and that is how God would answer as well.

At this point, Jesus lets his listeners draw the most important and startling conclusions. If he, Jesus, acts this way with sinners and the lost and if what he is doing—as has just been revealed—is the same way that God acts, then Jesus is like God, and Jesus is God! That is exactly what Jesus intended to say. The context of the parables of mercy is *christological*: they speak about Christ, about his transcendent person and mission. They are a proclamation about him, with an authoritativeness that is so much more effective because it is made less explicit—without direct explanations and entrusted uniquely to the intelligence of whoever hears. (The best conclusions are always the ones that people come to by themselves!) It is like the time Jesus healed the paralytic (see Luke 5:17ff) but first said, "Man, your sins are forgiven" (5:20). Suddenly everyone around him said, "But only God can do that!" (see 5:21), and he responded calmly by healing the paralytic and forcing them to draw their own logical conclusion about the event.

2. Joy and Hope in God's Heart

We will not lay out each of the three parables here; it is clear, however, that they cannot be isolated in such a way as to be considered separately since all three are strictly linked. They are told together as if in a single breath with no interruptions: a certain shepherd has one hundred sheep . . . or a woman has ten drachmas . . . or a father has two sons.

However, we can look at the three parables as they file before us in procession and catch the dominant note of their lullaby. That dominant note (the protagonists of the parables!) is not the lost sheep, the lost drachma, or the prodigal son. It is true that these titles have been ascribed to these parables by tradition, but they are unauthorized titles given only for convenience. These parables of mercy do not actually speak mainly about people or sinners but about God. Even more precisely, about the joy of God!

If the context is christological, the text of these parables is *theological*. In other words, they contain a revelation about God, a striking revelation. If mercy and love (*hesed*) are the characteristic traits of God throughout the Old Testament, then we need to say that these parables constitute the high noon of biblical revelation about God. Moreover, they add something that was not known before, at least in such a clear way: God *enjoys* having mercy! The prophet Micah had said that God "does not retain his anger for ever because he *delights* in steadfast love [italics added]" (7:18). This concept, spoken of in a "muted" way before, is now being shouted from the rooftops.

Let us go back to the heart of these parables, God's joy. It is mentioned three times in the very short parable of the shepherd: having found the lost sheep, he comes home "*rejoicing*"; he tells his friends, "*Rejoice with me*," and "*there will be more joy* in heaven" (Luke 15:5-7; italics added). In the parable of the good father, his joy overflows and leads him to prepare a feast. He is beside himself with joy and hardly knows what to do next: he brings out luxurious clothes, the ring with the family seal (something that in antiquity was honored as a sign of distinction), and the fatted calf. He forgets his age and dignity and starts to run like a child ("his father saw him and . . . ran" [Luke 15:20]) and cries out to everyone, "Let's have a feast! We need to celebrate!"

These parables have the cheeriest air in the world, but when we think them over for a bit, deep down they bring up first an unsettling question and then a real temptation. The shepherd's joy is understandable, but why "more joy" for the lost sheep than for the ninety-nine sheep who caused no problem? Aren't we all children of God in the same way? So then why is one sheep worth ninety-nine other sheep, and above all, why is the one who wandered off and was worth the least now valued more? Isn't all of this a bit much?

I have found the best and most persuasive answer to this objection not in exegetical Gospel commentaries but in the theological poet Charles Péguy. He says that in getting lost, the sheep, just like the younger son, made God's very heart tremble; God was afraid of losing it forever and of being forced to condemn it and thus be deprived of it for all eternity. He feared this, and that fear caused hope in God's heart, and his hope, once fulfilled, caused joy and a feast:

. . . The fact is that a man's repentance

Is the crowning of one of God's hopes. . . .

The anxious expectation, the hope of this repentance

Has made hope well up in the heart of God, . . .

Has caused to spring forth, to arise something

   like an unknown feeling in the very heart of God, . . .

Of God who is eternally new.

And this very repentance

Was for him, in him, the crowning of a hope.

For all the others God loves in love.

But this sheep Jesus loves also in hope.[40]

In loving us, God put himself in the position of having to hope for something from us, even from the greatest sinner. This is a stunningly new thing; it is a reversal of everything. Who could have imagined it? We do not know, of course, how God's hope works; even in human beings this sentiment is so very subtle, elusive, and mysterious. We can at least say that God's hope does not depend on knowing the outcome of his expectation; it depends on not wanting it without a person's freedom. For us the condition that allows for hope is the future; for God it is a person's free will.

Years ago there was a case that riveted Italy. A two-year-old girl was missing, and for some time no one knew anything about what

---

[40] Charles Péguy, *The Portico of the Mystery of the Second Virtue* [*La porche de la deuxième vertue*], trans. Dorothy Brown Aspinwall (Metuchen, NJ: Scarecrow, 1970), p. 91.

had happened to her. Very troubling scenarios were suggested; the parents were in despair. On the third day the child suddenly reappeared, and the television cameras that were closely following the story caught the very moment when the mother, seeing the child, ran over to her, picked her up, hugged her, and covered her with kisses. It was the very picture of happiness. In watching this scene, I said to myself, "This is what Jesus was saying when he talked about the joy of God for a child that was found!" I am sure that had they been able to choose, the mother and father would have preferred for the child never to have gotten lost (and God would have felt the same). But once it happened, finding her again brought them a joy they would never have known if nothing had happened to her in the first place. For them as well, the agony had birthed hope, and that hope, once fulfilled, made their joy explode.

Something similar happened with the death and resurrection of Jesus. (The father in the parable says, "My son was dead, and is alive again" [Luke 15:24]). No matter how dull we are, can we really think that the Father was idle and without expectation during the time between Jesus' death and his resurrection? When Jesus was resurrected, it caused excessive joy for the Father, much greater than if Jesus had not died and been raised. That is the case with the sheep and the prodigal son.

I said we do not know how God's hope works, but just knowing that God hopes for something from us should not leave us tranquil but put wings on our hearts. We are able to crown (or fail to crown) an expectation by God! In one of his novels, Dostoevsky describes a scene that seems to capture an event that was actually observed. A peasant woman is holding a baby that is a few weeks old when for the first time, according to her, the baby smiles. She humbly makes the Sign of the Cross, and when someone asks her why she did that, she answers, "There is joy for a mother in her child's first smile, just as God rejoices when from heaven he sees a sinner praying to him with his whole heart."[41]

The sinner who reads the three parables of Jesus can be touched by them and decide to convert for many reasons. They are haunting words that seep into us like water; they act on our minds, our hearts, our imagination, our memory. They know how to pull at our heartstrings and touch various chords: regret, shame ("He would gladly have fed on the pods that the swine ate" [Luke 15:16]), nostalgia ("My father's hired servants have bread enough" [15:17]). Only God knows how many people have been touched by these parables. Those of us who are priests have some indication. Rarely are these parables proclaimed to people in the course of spiritual exercises, a mission, or a retreat without something significant happening to someone, some genuine melting. The parables' power is thus always intact and ever new. I said whoever reads them can be touched and may decide to convert for various reasons. However, the best reason to convert is suggested by Jesus: "God is waiting for something from me, and I want to make him happy!"

---

[41] Fyodor Dostoevsky, *The Idiot*, trans. Henry and Olga Carlisle (New York: New American Library, 1969), p. 240.

There is a statement by Jesus quoted by St. Paul that says, "It is more blessed to give than to receive" (Acts 20:35). We know that this is true for God as well, and for God above all. God's love is characteristically and absolutely free. There is therefore "more joy" in heaven for a converted sinner because it allows God to forgive, and forgiving is like giving twice: it allows him to love in his own way, which is to love us "first" (see 1 John 4:19)—to be the first to love every time, with a love not based on reciprocation.

3. And the Older Son?

Now we can tackle the thorniest problem in these parables. I have said that they are without problems only on the surface. Like all of God's words, they are actually full of mysterious ravines and deep abysses. Here is the problem: what about the other ninety-nine sheep and the older brother in the parable? Are they excluded from this stupendous possibility of making God happy? Are they discriminated against and consigned to a kind of lower status in relation to God and the spiritual life?

This is not a rhetorical objection. When I was explaining the gospel on Saturday night years ago on the television program *In His Image* on the channel *Rai Uno*, I commented once on the so-called parable of the prodigal son. Afterward a listener wrote me the following:

Contrary to the traditional interpretation, I believe the prodigal son was essentially a rascal and a hypocrite. A slacker, stupidly frittering away the money he had claimed from his father. Then when he was hungry he said to himself, "Even servants are well treated in my father's house, so I will get up and tell my father I have sinned against heaven and against him." . . . His motivation was not repentance but hunger. He went home through necessity and not because of love. The other son is not likable, but he is not a hypocrite, and unlike his brother he does not act in an arrogant and foolish way. Instead he has worked for years; he never even took time for a night of celebration and festivity. His grumpy attitude can be annoying, but between the two brothers, frankly I prefer the integrity, although it is limited, of the older son rather than the inane and questionable arrogance of the son who left home.

This viewer's reaction is enough to make us see that the parable is not really logical and cannot be understood unless we enter into God's thoughts, which are so different from ours. Let us, first of all, remove a confusing side issue. The fact that there is "more joy" in heaven for a repentant sinner does not mean that the sinner now has more holiness or more merit or more glory with respect to the righteous. That has nothing to do with it. The parable is dealing with a fact about God, not the sinner.

Here is an answer that matters more. For the righteous (genuinely righteous, however!), there is something better: taking part in God's joy! What does the shepherd say to his friends and the woman to her friends? *Rejoice with me!* What does the father say to the elder brother? "Let us eat and make merry" (Luke 15:23)—meaning "you and I"—because the brother has returned; he also tells him, "All that is mine is yours" (15:31). The father is saying, "Both my anxiety and hope should have been yours, and now my joy should be yours because this is about your brother!"

This is the "second mountain peak" of the three parables. Jesus' goal was to tell the scribes and Pharisees that their attitude toward sinners constituted not only a criticism against God—God takes no pleasure in the death of the wicked but wants them to convert and live (see Ezekiel 18:23)—but also constituted an insult to their neighbor. They were trespassing, then, against both the first and second great commandments. A brother cannot remain indifferent to a younger brother who leaves home; he should suffer with his father, and if the brother returns, he should rejoice with the father.

The three parables, which aimed at talking to us only about God, end up, then, talking about everybody and to everybody, indiscriminately: the sinners and the righteous; those far away and those nearby. However, I would caution whoever hears these parables against quickly identifying themselves with those who remain in the sheepfold and who "need no repentance" (Luke 15:7). In fact, I have a terrible suspicion that Jesus' words about those who "need no repentance," implying that they are already righteous, do not have an *objective* meaning but instead a *subjective* and ironic meaning: "those who '*feel* no need' for repentance."

Who can actually think they do not need conversion and a return to God? The scribes and Pharisees thought that way about themselves, but we know how things really were. The sheep who are the most lost, the sons who have gone the farthest away and are in most need of returning, are precisely the ones who have gone astray in their own arrogance, who have entrenched themselves in their own righteousness and observance of the law, like the Pharisee who was praying in the Temple. Among other things, going "into a far country" (Luke 15:13), like the younger son did, does not mean committing great, unforgivable sins, resulting in a resounding break with faith and with the Church. A person can go far away all at once with a single giant step but also with small steps a little at a time, one compromise today, another tomorrow; one omission today, another tomorrow.

The parables of mercy, then, are for everybody. No one is excluded from the need for conversion, so for that very reason, no one is excluded from the extraordinary possibility of crowning a hope in God, of making God happy, of taking part in his happiness. As long as we are here on earth, the two roles—of the younger son and the older son—will never stop alternating for us.

What can we deduce for our lives from this "simultaneous" reading of the three parables? This, above all: God really loves us; whatever has to do with us, what happens to us, does not leave him indifferent but echoes in his heart to the point of causing him anxiety, hope, sorrow, and joy. We must be truly precious to him!

Second, we can deduce that we are precious to him as individuals, not as a group of people or just as numbers. The fact that he focuses on a single sheep and puts it before all the rest of the flock functions to emphasize precisely the point that God knows us by name; each of us is a son or a daughter who is unique and unrepeatable for him. God knows how to count only to one, and that "one" is each person! Isn't this fundamentally what every good father or mother does on earth? If a mother has five children, she does not divide her love into five parts to portion out a little bit for each child; she loves each child with all the love she has.

The three parables of mercy contain a message for all of us. For us priests, we are reminded of our duty to go in search of lost sheep and welcome them with mercy when they return. For the many prodigal sons today who stray far away and waste their parental means in "loose living" (Luke 15:13), the parables make us glimpse the possibility of a radical change and a different life, without the bitter taste of "pods for swine" in our mouths. They encourage mothers and fathers who have children who are "straying" to be patient and hopeful toward them in view of the patience and hope that God has for each of us (and that he perhaps had with them when they were young themselves!).

Everyone can find in the parables the part that is up to them to actualize in their own lives.

Chapter 10

"For our sake he made him to be sin"
The Passion of Christ,
the Height of God's Mercy

1. A Leap in Quality

In the first chapter, we saw the form that God's love takes after humanity's sin: forgiveness, and with it suffering. Love becomes "love with passion," that is, having pain in some way. This pain, as I said, does not occur only at the moment in which the Word becomes flesh and "devises his own self-emptying."[42] A "passion of love" existed in God much earlier, and it produced "the wonderful economy of redemptive love in Jesus Christ,"[43] according to St. John Paul II. In other words, God's passion precedes the Incarnation.

It is certain, however, that in the passion of Christ, God's suffering undergoes a leap in quality, because it, too, "was incarnated" and became a historical reality in space and time. It becomes a kind of suffering that is well known to us, that speaks to us in a direct way from within our history. The very topic of God's suffering is what we should now pause to consider in devout meditation. There

---

[42] See Cabasilas, VI, 3, p. 163.
[43] John Paul II, *Dominum et vivificantem* [On the Holy Spirit in the Life of the Church and the World], n. 39.

is no better school in which we can learn about God's mercy than standing before the Crucified One.

The great innovation that Christ's passion brought in regard to God's mercy is that God was not satisfied with forgiving people's sins. He did infinitely more than that: he took them upon himself; he shouldered them himself. This is what God had earlier announced and promised through the figure of the Suffering Servant of Yahweh (see Isaiah 53:4). In his book *Jesus of Nazareth*, Pope Benedict XVI wrote, "That which is wrong, the reality of evil, cannot simply be ignored; it cannot just be left to stand. It must be dealt with; it must be overcome. Only this counts as a true mercy. And the fact that God now confronts evil himself because men are incapable of doing so—therein lies the 'unconditional' goodness of God."[44]

The correct understanding of Christ's passion can be hindered by viewing the situation from what it could look like externally, that is, with people and their sin on one side and Jesus on the other side as he suffers and expiates the penalty for those sins while remaining at a distance, intact. The relationship between Jesus and sinners, however, is not distant, indirect, and merely legal; it is close and real. Sins, in other words, were placed on him; he saddled himself with them because he freely "carried them on his back," so to speak: "He himself bore our sins in his body" (1 Peter 2:24), in himself. He felt in some way as though he were the sin

---

[44] Joseph Ratzinger [Benedict XVI], *Jesus of Nazareth, Part II* (San Francisco: Ignatius Press, 2011), p. 133.

of the world. "For our sake he made him to be sin who knew no sin, so that in him we might become the righteousness of God" (2 Corinthians 5:21).

2. "Unjust" Suffering

After sin occurred, the greatness of a human being before God is in bearing the least possible *guilt* and the most possible *punishment* for sin—in other words, in being "a lamb" (a victim) and being "spotless" (innocent). That greatness lies not so much in each thing separately—suffering or innocence—as it does in the synthesis of these two characteristics and their coexistence in the same person. The highest value, then, is the suffering of the innocent. Only Jesus of Nazareth is at the top of this new ladder of greatness, he whom Scripture defines specifically as the "lamb without blemish or spot" (1 Peter 1:19). Without ever having committed *any* sin, he carried *all* the penalty of sin: "He committed no sin . . . [but] he himself bore our sins" (2:22, 24).

To say that Jesus took upon himself the penalty of sin does not mean that he took only the *punishment* on himself but that he also took on something much worse, the *blame* for that very sin. He took sin on himself without having committed it. Human beings were made to be innocent, so guilt is repulsive to them more than suffering itself. No one wants to feel guilty; if at times people boast about their sins, it is because they have earlier inverted their values or found other justifications in their own minds so that what others consider sin, they consider worthy of merit or at least something they needed to do.

To some extent, we have all had the bitter experience of being accused of something, perhaps even in the eyes of a person whom we esteem and whose esteem we most value. And we have seen what that does to our hearts. We notice every day how hard it is to accept the blame openly—even if it is a minor thing and even if it is deserved—without trying to defend ourselves. We can understand, then, what depths are concealed behind the fact that Jesus was considered "answerable" to his Father for every sin in the world. Jesus experienced, to the highest degree, the most crushing, ingrained, and universal cause of human suffering, the "sense of guilt." Even that, however, is now redeemed at its root.

The greatest thing in the world, then, is not "just suffering" but "unjust suffering," as the First Letter of Peter says (see 2:19). It is so great and precious because it is the only thing that brings us close to God's mode of suffering. Only God, when he suffers, can ever, in a complete way, suffer innocently and unjustly. When people suffer, they should all say like the good thief on the cross, "We are suffering indeed justly" (see Luke 23:41)—if for no other reason than because of the solidarity that links them to the rest of sinful humanity. Only Jesus can say about himself in an absolute sense what the good thief said next: "This man has done nothing wrong" (23:41).

This is also the principal difference the Letter to the Hebrews notes between the sacrifice of Christ and that of every other priest. "He has no need . . . to offer sacrifices daily, first for his own sins and then for those of the people" (7:27). When people are suffering and have no sin of their own that needs expiation, their suffering is transformed into the pure power of expiation. Not bearing in themselves the sad marks of sin, the quality of their suffering is purer and their voices speak "more graciously than the blood of Abel" (12:24; see Genesis 4:10). The greatest and most insurmountable scandal in the eyes of the world—the suffering of the innocent—is for God the greatest wisdom and righteousness. It is a mystery, but that is the way it is, and on this issue God seems to be repeating to us what Jesus said in the Gospel one day: "He who is able to receive this, let him receive it" (Matthew 19:12).

3. "Father, forgive them!"

"Greater love has no man than this, that a man lay down his life for his friends," Jesus said at the Last Supper (John 15:13). We could exclaim, "But there does exist a greater love than giving one's life for one's friends: your love! You did not give your life for your friends but for your enemies!" Paul says that scarcely can someone be found who is ready to die for a just man, although such a man might be found: "But God shows his love for us in that while we were yet sinners Christ died for us" (Romans 5:8).

The word "friends" in the active sense indicates those who love you, but in the passive sense it indicates those whom you love. Jesus calls Judas "friend" (Matthew 26:50), not because Judas loved him, but because he loved Judas! There is no greater love than giving one's life for one's enemies while considering them friends; this is what Jesus meant by his statement. People can be—or act as though they are—enemies of God, but God will never be the enemy of any human being. That is the terrible advantage children have over their fathers and mothers.

Jesus died, crying out, "Father, forgive them; for they know not what they do" (Luke 23:34). This is not a prayer; it is a peremptory request made with the authority that comes from being the Son: "Father, forgive them!" And since Jesus said that the Father heard all his prayers (see John 11:42), we have to believe that the Father heard this last prayer from the cross as well. Consequently, the crucifiers of Christ were then forgiven by God (not, of course, without being repentant in some way) and are with him in paradise, to testify for all eternity to what extremes the love of God is capable of going.

Ignorance by itself existed exclusively among the soldiers. But Jesus' prayer is not limited to them. The divine magnanimity of his forgiveness consists in the fact that it was also offered to his most relentless enemies. The excuse of ignorance is brought forward precisely for them. Even though they acted with cunning and malice, they really did not know what they were doing; they did not think they were nailing a man to the cross who was actually the Messiah and the Son of God! Instead of accusing his adversaries or forgiving them but entrusting the task of vengeance to his heavenly Father, he defended them.

He presents his disciples with an example of infinite generosity. To forgive with his same greatness of soul does not entail just a negative attitude through which one renounces wishing evil on those who do evil; it has to be transformed, instead, into a positive will to do good to them, even if it is only through a prayer to God on their behalf. "Pray for those who persecute you" (Matthew 5:44). This kind of forgiveness cannot seek a reward in the hope of divine punishment. It must be inspired by a charity that excuses one's neighbor, without, however, closing one's eyes to the truth; on the contrary, it must seek to stop evildoers so they will not do any future harm to others and to themselves.

We might want to say, "Lord, you are asking us to do the impossible!" He would answer, "I know, but I died so that you could do what I am asking of you. I not only gave you the *command* to forgive and a heroic *example* of forgiveness, but through my death I also obtained for you the *grace* that enables you to forgive. I did not give the world merely a teaching on mercy as so many others have. I am God, and I have poured out rivers of mercy for you through my death. You may draw as much mercy as you want from those waters during the Jubilee Year of Mercy and at every moment."

The practice that I would most recommend during the Year of Mercy is to pick up a Gospel and read the account of the passion unhurriedly all the way through. It would take less than half an hour.

I knew an intellectual woman who professed to be an atheist. One day she got the kind of news that leaves people stunned: her sixteen-year-old daughter had a tumor in her rib cage. They operated, and she returned from the torment of the operating room with nasogastric tubes, drainage tubes, and intravenous feeding tubes coming out of her body. The girl was suffering horribly and groaning, and she did not want to hear any words of comfort. Knowing that her daughter was devoutly religious, and thinking that it would please her, the mother asked her, "Do you want me to read you something from the Gospel?" "Yes, Mama, read me the Gospel," she answered. "What do you want me to read you from the Gospel?" "Read me the passion." The mother, never having read the Gospel, ran to get a Bible from the hospital chaplains. She sat at her daughter's bedside and began to read. After a while, the girl fell asleep, but the mother continued to read silently in the semidarkness up to the end. She said in the book she wrote afterward that "the daughter fell asleep, but the mother woke up!" She woke up from her atheism. Her reading of the passion of Christ had changed her life forever.[45]

---

[45] See Rosanna Garofalo, *Sopra le ali dell'aquila* [On the Wings of the Eagle] (Milan: Ancora, 1993).

"He was raised for our justification"
THE RESURRECTION OF CHRIST AND THE VICTORY OF GOD'S MERCY

1. "O wonder of your humble care for us!"

At the beginning of the Easter vigil, the liturgy of the Church intones one of its most inspired and boldest songs, the *Exultet*:

> O wonder of your humble care for us!
> O love, O charity beyond all telling,
> to ransom a slave you gave away your Son!
> O truly necessary sin of Adam,
> destroyed completely by the Death of Christ!
> O happy fault
> that earned so great, so glorious a Redeemer!

God the Father responds to the greatest sin of the world—the killing of his Son—with his greatest act of mercy. Jesus was raised from the dead not "for our condemnation" but "for our justification" (see Romans 4:25). Phrases that indicate the cause of Jesus' death—"*because* of our trespasses," "*because* of us" (*propter nos*)—often become transformed in the passion texts into phrases

104

expressing the purpose: Jesus died *"for* our sake," *"for* our salvation" (*pro nobis*).

There is a simple but moving song on this point whose lyrics are accompanied by a stirring and very sweet melody:

Hallelujah, my Father
For giving us Your Son
Sending Him into the world
To be given up for men
Knowing we would bruise Him
And smite Him from the earth
Hallelujah, my Father
In His death is my birth
Hallelujah, my Father
In His life is my life.[46]

2. "Victor because victim"

How does Jesus act in his victory? Let us reflect on one characteristic of the resurrection that is not often considered very much: his humility. The victory of the resurrection occurs in mystery, without witnesses. His death was seen by a large crowd, but once risen, he appeared only to limited groups of witnesses away from crowds. The Roman historian Tacitus knows about his death but knows nothing about his resurrection. He knows that a certain "Christ"

---

[46] Tim Cullen, © 1975, Celebration/Kingsways Thankyou Music.

was put to death under Pontius Pilate,[47] but he does not know that Christ was raised and is alive. Jesus still remains for the "world" the condemned man, the man whose life ended on the cross.

The mysterious quality of the resurrection indicates that we do not need to expect an external, visible triumph—like some kind of earthly fame—after a person has suffered: the victory is given by God invisibly and on a higher level! The resurrection is sufficiently revealed through Christ's appearances to furnish a solid foundation for faith. However, it does not involve revenge to humiliate the adversaries; Jesus does not appear in their midst to demonstrate that they were mistaken and throw the wrong they did to him in their faces. Any vengeance would be incompatible with the love he wanted to demonstrate to human beings through his passion.

Jesus acts humbly in the glory of his resurrection, just as he did in his death on Calvary. That is the nature of a victory born from suffering. It is a supernatural victory insofar as it was a triumph of God and, consequently, a victory that can remain hidden on earth and has eternity for its setting.

In the paschal mystery of Christ, a new kind of victory is revealed that Augustine condenses into the phrase "*victor quia victima*," "victor because victim."[48] With Jesus we truly have what Friedrich Nietzsche defined as "the inversion of all values,"[49] but

---

[47] Tacitus, *Annals*, 15, 44.

[48] St. Augustine, *Confessions*, 10, 43.

[49] Friedrich Nietzsche, *Beyond Good and Evil*, ed. Rolf-Peter Horstmann, trans. Judith Norman (Cambridge, UK: Cambridge University Press, 2002), p. 84.

with a different meaning than the one he intended. For Nietzsche, the inversion of all values by the gospel is a negative thing. It reflects the impotent resentment of the weak against the strong, who represent the Apollonian and Dionysian pagan ideal of the magnanimous man full of health who aspires to great things and was born to overcome rather than be defeated. Our experience, even recently, demonstrates which of the two ideals is really worthy of human beings and can resolve conflicts.

With Jesus there truly was a total inversion of all values, but for our good, not for our disgrace. The idea of victory—for the first time, but in a definitive way—was separated from the idea of vengeance. It is only a question of seeing when the world will notice and draw conclusions about it.

But let us think about this. Why does the victory of mercy necessarily have to be discrete and humble? The answer is simple: because it is the victory of love, and there is no love without humility. We already understood that idea in the first chapter when we talked about God's visceral love. When it is genuine and total, love recoils from any revenge; it lets things be. The humility of love furnishes the key to understanding this. People do not need much effort to put themselves in the limelight, but on the other hand, it takes a lot of strength to step aside, to be self-effacing. God has an unlimited capacity for concealing himself, and the paschal mystery of the death and resurrection is the definitive revelation of that.

3. Two Ways of Representing Christ's Resurrection

In the light of what has been said, it seems evident that this characteristic of Christ's victory is better expressed in the Orthodox iconography than in Renaissance and later Western art. In Western art, the resurrection of Christ is an "ascent," while in Byzantine iconography it is a "descent." In the West we see a Christ who is triumphantly exiting the tomb, often rising upward to heaven and at times escorted by throngs of angels, while the men guarding the tomb are lying on the ground stunned or sleeping. In Eastern art the risen Jesus, surrounded by light, does not rise up but goes down into the darkness of the nether regions to bring back up with him Adam, Eve, and all the righteous waiting for redemption. It is a victory hidden from the eyes of the world, consistent with his kind of victory of love and mercy. This is how a text from the Byzantine liturgy describes the paschal mystery of Christ:

Today a sacred Pascha is revealed to us.

A new and holy Pascha, a mysterious Pascha. . . .

A Pascha that has opened the gates of paradise for us.

A Pascha that sanctifies the faithful.

This is Resurrection day. . . .

Let us radiate joy for this feast, let us embrace each other.

Let us call "brothers" even those who hate us

And forgive all because of the Resurrection.[50]

The resurrection is the school of mercy; it invites reconciliation and forgiveness of our enemies. I have always thought only one subject was worthy of the musical chorale that closes Beethoven's Ninth Symphony: the resurrection of Christ. Only that event could have constituted an adequate "text" for such sublime notes. And we find almost the same words of this Byzantine liturgical hymn written so many centuries ago in Friedrich Schiller's "Ode to Joy," which the composer set to music.

All men will become brothers
Where Joy's gentle wing hovers
Be embraced by Joy, you millions!
This kiss is for the whole world!

The difference with the joy sung in Schiller's ode is that it is only longed for; it does not exist. And if it did exist, it would be reserved only for a few, for those whose lot in life is to have a good spouse or to know the pleasure of drinking a glass of wine in the company of friends, as other verses of Schiller's ode say. The Easter hymn speaks instead of a joy fulfilled and offered to every person. Christ's resurrection is truly the victory of God's mercy.

---

[50] See the Orthodox Stichera, Hymns for Pascha, in Georges Gharib, *Le icone festive della Chiesa Ortodossa* (Milan: Ancora, 1985), pp. 174–182.

CHAPTER 12

"The righteousness of God has been manifested!"
GOD'S JUSTICE AND MERCY

1. God Is Righteous in Showing Mercy

One of the problems about mercy that has been debated all along is its relationship to God's righteousness and justice. The problem was resolved once and for all by St. Paul, but people are not always aware of this when they speak about mercy. The brief answer is "justification by grace through faith."

The apostle begins his exposition with the news that "the righteousness of God has been manifested" (Romans 3:21). What righteousness? The righteousness that gives each person his or her due and distributes rewards and punishments according to merits? In brief, what do we mean by "righteousness"? It is true that there will be a time in which this kind of righteous justice from God will be manifested. The apostle, in fact, writes shortly before in Romans 2:6-8 that God "will render to every man according to his works: to those who by patience in well-doing seek for glory and honor and immortality, he will give eternal life; but for those who are factious and do not obey the truth, but obey wickedness, there will be wrath and fury."

But Paul is certainly not talking about this kind of justice when he writes, "The righteousness of God has been manifested." The first kind of justice he talks about involves a future event, but this one is occurring "now." If that were not the case, Paul's statement would be an absurd affirmation that contradicts the facts. From the perspective of distributive justice, nothing changed in the world with the coming of Christ. People still see the guilty in power and the innocent on the scaffold. The situation is at times reversed, with the innocent in power and the guilty on the scaffold, lest people should believe there is any kind of fixed order in the world. It is not, therefore, in those situations that we need to look for the innovation brought by Christ. Let us hear what the apostle says:

Since all have sinned and fall short of the glory of God, they are justified by his grace as a gift, through the redemption which is in Christ Jesus, whom God put forward as an expiation by his blood, to be received by faith. This was to show God's righteousness, because in his divine forbearance he had passed over former sins; it was to prove at the present time that he himself is righteous and that he justifies him who has faith in Jesus. (Romans 3:23-26)

God shows his righteous justice in having mercy! This is the great revelation, this is the "vengeance" of God on people who have sinned. The apostle says God is "just and justifying"; that is, he is just to himself when he justifies human beings. He is, in fact, love and mercy, so for that reason he is just to himself—he truly demonstrates who he is—when he has mercy.

But none of this makes sense if we cannot understand exactly what the expression "the righteousness of God" means. There is a danger that people can hear talk about the righteousness of God but not know its significance, so instead of being encouraged, they are frightened and think to themselves, "Look, that's just what we expected; after the wrath of God, now his 'righteousness' is also manifested, and that means his just punishment!"

It was Luther who discovered, or better, rediscovered, that the phrase "the righteousness of God" does not indicate his punishment of people—or worse, his vengeance against them. On the contrary, it indicates the action through which God in his infinite mercy "made people righteous." (Luther actually said "declare" and not "made" just because he was thinking of an extrinsic and forensic justification.) He later wrote that when he discovered this, "I felt that I was altogether born again and had entered paradise itself through open gates."[51]

I said Luther "rediscovered" this because St. Augustine before him had clearly explained the meaning of the phrase "the righteousness of God" according to Paul's use of it: "'The righteousness of God' is that by which we are made righteous, just as 'the salvation

---

[51] Martin Luther, *Preface to Latin Writings*, in *Luther's Works*, vol. 34 (Philadelphia: Fortress Press, 1960), p. 337.

of God' (Psalm 3:4) means the salvation by which he causes us to be saved."[52]

The "gospel," the good news, that St. Paul brings to the Christians in Rome is this: God's kindness is now manifested to human beings, his goodwill toward human beings, his forgiveness, in a word, his mercy. Scripture explains the concept of the "righteousness of God" this way: "When the goodness and loving kindness of God our Savior appeared, he saved us, not because of deeds done by us in righteousness, but in virtue of his own mercy" (Titus 3:4-5). Elsewhere, Paul says, "God, who is rich in mercy, out of the great love with which he loved us, even when we were dead through our own trespasses, made us alive together with Christ (by grace you have been saved)" (see Ephesians 2:4-5).

To say that "the righteousness of God has been manifested" is like saying that God's goodness, his love, and his mercy have been revealed. God's justice not only does not contradict his mercy but consists precisely in mercy!

2. A Message Born from Experience

The apostle Paul did not invent this new, revolutionary message himself. If that were the case, people who say that he, not Jesus, is the real founder of Christianity would be right. But that is not

---

[52] Augustine, *The Spirit and the Letter*, 32, 56, PL 44, p. 237; see *Augustine: Later Works*, trans. and intro. John Burnaby (Philadelphia: Westminster Press, 1955), p. 241.

the case. Paul says the gospel "is the power of God for salvation to every one who has faith" (Romans 1:16). He speaks about the time of "divine forbearance" that has been fulfilled and of the righteousness of God that has come "at the present time" and manifests itself (3:25ff). What other words sound like these? Who reminds us of this kind of language? These words remind us of the words of Jesus who, at the beginning of his ministry, went about proclaiming, "The time is fulfilled, and the kingdom of God is at hand; repent, and believe in the gospel" (Mark 1:15).

Paul is transmitting to us the purest teaching of Jesus. What Christ means by the phrase "kingdom of God"—which is God's salvific initiative, his freely undertaken action on behalf of human beings—St. Paul calls "the righteousness of God," but both phrases concern the same fundamental reality, the same action of God.

When Jesus said, "Repent, and believe in the gospel," he was already teaching justification by faith. Before Jesus, "to convert" meant "to turn back" (which is what the Hebrew word *shub* means). It meant to turn back to the broken covenant through a renewed observance of the law. The Lord says through the prophet Zechariah, "Return to me. . . . Return from your evil ways and from your evil deeds" (1:3, 4; see also Jeremiah 8:4-5).

With Jesus, however, this ascetic and moral meaning moves to a second level (at least at the beginning of his preaching) and takes on a new meaning that had been unknown until this point. And only with Jesus could the word "conversion" assume this new meaning. Converting no longer means turning back to the old covenant and the observance of the law; it means taking a leap forward, entering a new covenant, seizing the kingdom that has now appeared and entering into it. And entering into it by faith. "Repent, and believe in the gospel" does not mean two different things that occur successively but refers to one single action: to repent means to believe—repent by believing!

God himself has taken the initiative for salvation, and he has made his kingdom come. People only need to welcome God's offer by faith and then live its requirements. This is why Jesus insists so much on receiving the kingdom "like a child" (Mark 10:15). A child never thinks of having to pay for what he asks his parents for.

3. Witnesses of Mercy

Where did the apostle get his message that people become righteous through mercy and not through merit? Not from the Gospels because they had not yet been written! If anything, Paul received it from the oral traditions of Jesus' preaching but especially from his own personal experience, from the way in which God had acted in his life. Writing to the Philippians, he explains his conversion as going from "having a righteousness of my own" to "the righteousness from God that depends on faith" (3:9).

Paul will not cease considering himself a result and a victory of God's mercy throughout his whole life. He defines himself as "one who has the mercy of the Lord" (see 1 Corinthians 7:25). He does not stop at formulating the doctrine of mercy but becomes a living witness to it: "I formerly blasphemed and persecuted and insulted him; but I received mercy because I had acted ignorantly in unbelief. . . . I received mercy for this reason, that in me, as the foremost, Jesus Christ might display his perfect patience for an example to those who were to believe in him for eternal life" (1 Timothy 1:13, 16). When he wants to exhort the faithful by the holiest thing in the universe, Paul exhorts them "by the mercies of God" (Romans 12:1).

Through this, the apostle teaches us that the best way to preach mercy is to give testimony to the mercy that God has shown toward us. We too should perceive ourselves as the fruit of God's mercy for us in Christ Jesus, and we live only because of his mercy. One day Jesus healed an unfortunate man possessed by an unclean spirit. He wanted to follow Jesus and the group of his disciples who were accompanying him as he traveled around. Jesus did not allow him to do that but said to him, "'Go home to your friends, and tell them how much the Lord has done for you, and how he has had mercy on you.' And he went away and began to proclaim in the Decapolis how much Jesus had done for him; and all men marveled" (Mark 5:19-20). This same kind of intention spurred Augustine to write his *Confessions*. Innumerable conversions happen today simply when people listen to stories of other people's lives and see what God's mercy has done for them. Personal testimony about how the Lord has worked in one's life, when it is humble and inspired by a desire to give God glory, is one of the most effective forms of evangelization.

CHAPTER 13

"Your sins are forgiven"
THE SACRAMENT OF MERCY

1. "Who can forgive sins but God alone?"

The mercy of God, as we have seen, involves far more than the simple forgiveness of sins. It is true, though, that forgiveness is the principal purpose of mercy, so to speak, and its greatest manifestation. In going from the Old to the New Testament, we also see a leap in quality in regard to forgiveness. With the coming of the Word into our midst, the forgiveness of God is also "made flesh"; it is manifested through concrete words and actions, first in Christ's life and then in the Church's sacraments. It is no longer proclaimed "through the prophets" but is directly given to us in first person by God himself.

At no time in the Gospel does this innovation appear with more clarity than in the episode of the paralytic lowered from the roof (see Mark 2:1-12). One day people heard that Jesus "was at home" (2:1). This almost certainly indicates Simon Peter's house because that was Jesus' "home" when he was in Capernaum. Such a large crowd gathered that there was no way for anyone to enter through the door. A group of people who had a relative or a friend who was paralyzed solved that problem by opening up the roof and lowering the sick man on his pallet before Jesus. The event is quite credible if we think about the Palestinian homes at the time (and still some today) that have only one floor and a roof of wood and clay. Seeing their faith, Jesus said to the paralytic, "My son, your sins are forgiven" (2:5). Some of the scribes present were scandalized and said to themselves, "It is blasphemy! Who can forgive sins but God alone?" (2:7).

Let us hear the rest of this Gospel passage directly:

> And immediately Jesus, perceiving in his spirit that they thus questioned within themselves, said to them, "Why do you question thus in your hearts? Which is easier, to say to the paralytic, 'Your sins are forgiven,' or to say, 'Rise, take up your pallet and walk'? But that you may know that the Son of man has authority on earth to forgive sins"—he said to the paralytic—"I say to you, rise, take up your pallet and go home." (Mark 2:8-11)

Jesus does not contradict their assertion that only God can forgive sins, but the miracle demonstrates to them that he has the same power on earth as God. People can "commit" sin, but only God can "remit" it. To think otherwise would be like saying that debtors, on their own initiative, can cancel a debt they owe someone! This has been the claim of modern human beings who end up saying, "I who accused myself today, I alone absolve myself."[53]

---

[53] See Jean-Paul Sartre, *The Devil and the Good Lord and Two Other Plays*, trans. Kitty Black (New York: Vintage Books, 1962), p. 141.

2. Why Confess Our Sins?

Jesus wanted the exercise of his power to remit sins not to be limited to the brief time of his earthly life. He therefore instituted a sacrament in which the Holy Spirit, through the ministry of the Church, continues to remit sins. The origin of this sacrament—apart from its innumerable changes and adjustments in history—is, in fact, a word of Christ addressed first only to Peter (see Matthew 16:19) and then collectively to all the apostles: "Receive the Holy Spirit. If you forgive the sins of any, they are forgiven; if you retain the sins of any, they are retained" (John 20:22-23).

There are many ways in which Christ continues this work of remitting sins. The Church has always recognized a general efficacy of deliverance from sin in the Eucharist. "Every time you drink this blood," writes St. Ambrose, "you receive the remission of sins and become inebriated with the Spirit"; he also states, "This bread is the remission of sins."[54] At the precise moment of the distribution of the Body of Christ in Communion, the liturgy reminds us of this truth, saying, "Behold the Lamb of God, behold him who takes away the sins of the world."

There is, however, a specific means that people are obliged to use when there is a question of a serious break in their relationship with God: the Sacrament of Penance. The Fathers call it the second "plank of salvation" for anyone "who is shipwrecked" after

---

[54] St. Ambrose, *On the Sacraments*, V, 3, 17, CSEL 73, p. 65; see also *The Blessings of the Patriarchs*, 9, 39, CSEL 32, 2, p. 147.

baptism.[55] According to Blessed Isaac of Stella, "The Church can forgive nothing without Christ, and Christ does not want to forgive anything except with the Church. The Church can forgive only a penitent, that is, a person whom Christ has touched with his grace, and Christ does not consider anyone who scorns the help of the Church forgiven."[56]

The one who remits sins is not the Church but the Holy Spirit. The Church is only exercising a ministry, but an indispensable ministry, in this case. Jesus said to the apostles, "If you forgive the sins of any, they are forgiven," but how can the apostles and their successors decide whether to remit sins without knowing what they are?

The method chosen by God to remit sins, which occurs through Confession, actually corresponds to a very natural and deep need of the human psyche. The practice of psychoanalysis itself is based on this fact and constitutes an unintentional confirmation of it and, at times, a substitute for it. The path of freeing oneself from sin by confessing it to God through his minister corresponds to the natural need in the human psyche to free oneself of what is weighing on one's conscience by exposing it, bringing it into the light, and verbally expressing it. Psalm 32 describes the joy that arises from that experience:

---

[55] Tertullian, "On Penitence," 4, 2; in *Treatises on Penance*, trans. and notes William P. Le Saint (Westminster, MD: Newman Press, 1959), p. 20; see also "On Penitence," 12, 9, where he calls Penance "a second safeguard," p. 36; see *CCL* I, pp. 326, 340.

[56] Blessed Isaac of Stella, "Sermon 11," *PL* 194, 1729.

Blessed is he whose transgression is forgiven,
  whose sin is covered. . . .
When I declared not my sin, my body wasted away
  through my groaning all day long. . . .
I acknowledged my sin to thee,
  and I did not hide my iniquity;
I said, "I will confess my transgressions to the LORD";
  then thou didst forgive the guilt of my sin. (Psalm 32:1, 3, 5)

Confession is the moment in which the dignity of the individual believer is most clearly confirmed. At every other time in the life of the Church, the believer is one among many: one among many who hear the word, one among many who receive the Eucharist. In the confessional, however, the believer is unique and alone; the Church exists only for him or her in that moment.

Confession allows us to experience for ourselves what the Church sings in the *Exultet* at the Easter vigil: "O happy fault that earned so great, so glorious a Redeemer!" Jesus knows how to take all our sins, once they are acknowledged, and make them "happy faults," faults that are no longer remembered except for the experience of mercy and tenderness they have occasioned!

3. Mercy and Repentance

Our manner of approaching the Sacrament of Penance must be renewed in the Spirit to become truly efficacious and decisive in the struggle against sin. To renew this sacrament in the Spirit means to approach it not as a ritual, a habit, or an obligation but as a need for the soul, as a personal encounter with the risen Christ who, through the Church, communicates to us the healing power of his blood and brings us the "joy and gladness" of being saved (Psalm 51:8).

Whenever people turn back to God in a major way, it is always concluded, at least in the Catholic Church, by making their confession, which restores people and gives them the sensation of literally being reborn. A good example of this can be seen in the life of French poet Charles Baudelaire, the author of *The Flowers of Evil*. During his life people considered him—as he himself did—a typical case of a "prodigal son." The person who stood in the place of the welcoming and loving father was his mother. It was to her home in the end that he returned ill, with his body like "a place laid waste"[57] because of his excesses. His mother, who had nursed him with endless dedication, was at his side when he died on August 31, 1867, after having made his confession and having requested and received the Last Rites "in full lucidity."

The mercy of God, whether in the Sacrament of Reconciliation or apart from it, does not have conditions, but it does require a sinner's repentance. Without repentance, mercy is not possible. To pretend otherwise would mean "getting away scot-free" with God, but it is written, "Do not be deceived; God is not mocked,

---

[57] Charles Baudelaire, "Monologue," *The Flowers of Evil*, 55 ["Causerie," *Les fleurs du mal*, 55], in *The Complete Verse*, vol. 1, trans. and ed. Francis Scarfe (London: Anvil Press Poetry, 1986), p. 130.

for whatever a man sows, that he will also reap" (Galatians 6:7). In his omnipotence God can do all but one thing: he cannot, on his own, make a heart become "broken and contrite" (Psalm 51:17). To do that he needs the consent of our free will. This is not actually a condition but a limitation God placed on himself when he created us as free beings.

He can invite someone by his grace and knock at the door, but he will not break it down if the person has barricaded himself or herself inside by rejecting him. The real obstacle to God's mercy is not the gravity of a person's sin but the hardening of a person's heart, an "unrepentant heart." Psalm 51, the *Miserere*, says, "Have mercy on me, O God, according to thy steadfast love; / according to thy abundant mercy blot out my transgressions," but then the sinner immediately adds, "For I know my transgressions. . . . / Against thee, thee only, have I sinned, / and done that which is evil in thy sight" (Psalm 51:1, 3, 4).

Evil cannot be simply ignored or covered over. It has to be destroyed, and that does not happen unless people assume responsibility for it and "claim" it as their own. God cannot do this; sinners have to do it. In acknowledging their own sin, people are proclaiming that God is innocent and admitting the truth that "wickedness suppresses" (see Romans 1:18). That is the miraculous power of acknowledging sin.

4. Penitents and Confessors

It is important that priests genuinely dispense Christ's mercy in this sacrament. The Latin Church has sought to explain this sacrament with the concept of a legal process from which one leaves acquitted or not acquitted, so according to this perspective, the minister is performing the function of a judge. If this view is the only one emphasized, it can have negative consequences because it becomes difficult to recognize Jesus' action through the confessor. In the parable of the prodigal son, the father does not act like a judge but exactly like a father. Even before the son has finished confessing his sin, the father embraces him and orders a feast. The gospel is the true "manual for confessors"; canon law can be of service to it but cannot be a substitute for it.

Jesus does not begin by asking the adulterous woman, Zacchaeus, or the other sinners he meets "the number and kind" of their sins in a high-handed manner: "How many times? With whom? Where?" He is concerned above all that the person experience mercy, tenderness, and even God's joy in welcoming a sinner. He knows that after this experience, the sinner will feel the need for a confession of sin that is increasingly complete. Throughout the Bible, we see God's pedagogic manner of not demanding everything all at once from people concerning issues of morality but only what they are able to understand at the moment. Paul speaks about "divine forbearance" (Romans 3:25) in this regard. The essential thing is that there is the beginning of a genuine repentance and a willingness to change and make amends for wrongdoing.

Francis of Assisi was as rigorous and merciless with himself as he was merciful with his brothers. He gave a recommendation to a superior in his order that applies to all confessors: "There should not be any brother in the world who has sinned, however much he may have possibly sinned, who, after he has looked into your eyes, would go away without having received your mercy, if he was looking for mercy. And if he were not to seek mercy, you should ask him if he wants mercy. And if he still sins thereafter a thousand times before your very eyes, love him more than me so that you may draw him back to the Lord. Always be merciful to such as these."[58]

In 1983, when the Synod of Bishops on Penance and Reconciliation in the Mission of the Church was in session, St. John Paul II proclaimed before the whole synod the sainthood of Blessed Leopoldo Mandić, the humble Capuchin who had spent his life hearing confession. St. Leopoldo was well known for his affability, his love, and the encouragement with which he welcomed all penitents and sent them home. If anyone reproved him for being "too good" and told him that God would ask him about his excessive leniency with penitents, he would answer, "We are not the ones who died for souls, but Jesus poured out his divine blood for them. We should treat souls, then, the way Jesus taught us by

---

[58] See St. Francis of Assisi, "Letter to a Minister," in *Frances and Clare: The Complete Works*, trans. and intro. Regis J. Armstrong and Ignatius C. Brady (New York: Paulist Press, 1982), p. 75.

his example. If the Lord reproaches me for too much leniency, I will say to him, 'Blessed Lord, You gave me that bad example.'"[59]

It is true that in addition to St. Leopoldo, who was very tenderhearted in Confession, there was another priest in the same Capuchin order, St. Pio of Pietrelcina, who was known for his occasionally rough ways of receiving and dismissing penitents, sometimes without absolution. But to imitate him in doing that, we would need to be sure of having his gift of establishing a close connection with souls and of having them return to his confessional immediately afterward with their hearts changed.

Administering penance can become an occasion of conversion and grace for a confessor, just as it can for a preacher who proclaims the word. The sins confessed by a penitent can make a confessor easily recognize his own sins, although in different forms, so while he is hearing a confession, he can at least say to himself, "Lord, I too, I too have done that. Have mercy on me too." How many sins that are never included in our examination of conscience come to light in listening to the sins of others! To the most dejected penitents, St. Leopoldo would encourage them by saying, "We are two sinners; may God have mercy on both of us!"[60]

---

[59] Quoted in Lorenzo da Fara, *Leopoldo Mandić: L'umanità, la santità* (Padua: Opera san Leopoldo Mandić, 1987), pp. 103–104. For the life of this saint, see Pietro E. Bernadi, *Leopoldo Mandić: Saint of the Reconciliation* (Padua: Sanctuary of St. Leopoldo Mandić, 1989).
[60] Ibid., p. 106.

Let us end this meditation with a section of poetry by Paul Claudel that describes Confession using the same images with which the liturgy celebrates the resurrection of Christ:

My God, I have been revived and I am with You again!
I was sleeping, laid out like a dead person through the night.
God said, Let there be light! and I woke up
As a cry is uttered!
I rose up and I have awakened. . . .
My heart is free and my mouth is clear, my body and spirit
   are fasting.
I am absolved of all the sins I confessed, one by one.
The wedding ring is on my finger and my face is scrubbed clean.
I am like an innocent creature in the grace You have granted me.[61]

---

[61] Paul Claudel, *Corona benignitatis anni Dei*, in *Oeuvres poétiques* (Paris: Minard, 1976), p. 377.

CHAPTER 14

"With joy you will draw water from the wells of salvation"
THE MERCY OF GOD IN THE LITURGY

The holy Mass, which is the memorial of Christ's preaching in the Liturgy of the Word and the memorial of his death in the Eucharistic liturgy, is also consequently the memorial of God's mercy. It is the place where the mercy of Christ is not only recalled but received, experienced, and consumed. I will limit myself to noting some elements here and there that are most directly tied to the theme of mercy, first in the Mass and then in the liturgical year.

1. The Mercy of God in the Eucharistic Liturgy

Every holy Mass begins with the penitential rite. Its most ancient component, shared by all the rites and liturgies of the Church, is the invocation *"Kyrie eleison,"* proclaimed today in English as "Lord, have mercy." Unfortunately, however, like all things that are repeated an endless number of times, an understanding of the original content of this exclamation has been diminished.

What does *Kyrie eleison*, "Lord, have mercy!"—which punctuates Christian prayer and is added to the Mass in some liturgies from beginning to end—suggest to us? (Whoever has attended a Russian liturgy may recall how many times the invocation "*Gospodi pomiluj*" is repeated.) "Lord, have mercy on me," or "Have pity on me," has become for some people almost the only prayer they use to ask for forgiveness, believing that God is always ready to punish them. Unfortunately, the word "pity" has become so devalued that it is often used in a negative sense, as referring to bad and contemptible things: "something pitiful" or a "pitiful spectacle."

In line with biblical teaching, however, *Kyrie eleison* could be translated, "Lord, let the tenderness of your mercy come down upon us." We can see this in how God speaks about his people in Jeremiah: "My heart yearns for him; / I will surely have mercy on him, says the LORD" (Jeremiah 31:20). When the sick, the lepers, and the blind cry out to Jesus, "Have mercy [*eleeson*] on us, Son of David!" (Matthew 9:27), they do not mean, "Forgive us," but "Have compassion on us." Along with the forgiveness of sins, the conclusion of the penitential rite also assures us of mercy: "May almighty God have mercy on us, forgive us our sins, and bring us to everlasting life."

It is appropriate that the Roman liturgy has us repeat, "Lord, have mercy!" only at the beginning of the celebration. When someone gets to church on Sunday after having walked on dusty roads, he shakes the dust off his shoes before entering to try to remove every trace of dirt. But then, having done that, he does not spend the rest of his time looking at his shoes to see if there is still dirt on them; his attention is instead turned completely toward the altar where the great mystery is being celebrated. It would be foolish to do otherwise.

The Mass for the Twenty-sixth Sunday in Ordinary Time in the liturgical year opens with a prayer that Pope Francis quotes in his Bull for the Jubilee Year of Mercy: "[You] reveal your power above all in your mercy and forgiveness [*parcendo et miserando*]."[62] It is an assertion that has always attracted the attention of theologians because of its boldness. Forgiveness, perhaps even more so than creation, manifests God's omnipotence because it draws a human being out of a nothingness that is a deeper "nothing" than that of nonexistence. It draws a human being out of sin, which is what disconnects us from God, the source and cause of our being.

One way the liturgy gives us to celebrate God's mercy since the reform of the Second Vatican Council involves the two Eucharistic Prayers for Masses of Reconciliation. The first has as its theme "reconciliation as a return to the Father," and the second, "reconciliation with God as the foundation for peace among human beings." Each of them can offer a starting point for a comprehensive catechesis on God's mercy throughout the history of salvation. Among other things, in the first prayer we read, "Indeed, though we once were lost and could not approach you, you loved us with the greatest love [mercy]: for your Son, who alone is just, handed himself over to death, and did not disdain to be nailed for our sake to the wood of the Cross."

---

[62] *Misericordiae vultus*, n. 6.

2. The Feasts of Divine Mercy

Following his encyclical on God, *Dives in misericordia* [Rich in Mercy], published on November 30, 1980, St. John Paul II instituted the Feast of Divine Mercy, to be celebrated on the Sunday after Easter. The idea for the feast came from a private revelation by Jesus to St. Faustina Kowalska (1905–1938) and from the pious practices connected to it. I would like to try to describe the profound theological and pastoral meaning of this feast and the contribution it can bring right now to the vitality of the Church for a new evangelization.

In instituting the Feast of Corpus Christi, the Feast of the Sacred Heart of Jesus, and some other feasts, the Church received a message transmitted to some souls privately; it made the message its own and enriched it with theological content, placing it within the context of the whole of revelation and salvation history. The Church has done the same with the Feast of Divine Mercy. To understand the meaning John Paul II intended to give this feast, we need to take into account his encyclical no less than Jesus' revelations to St. Faustina.

What contribution has the magisterium made in this case? It has inserted christological devotion within the broader context of the Trinity. The God John Paul II describes as "rich in mercy" is not the person of Jesus taken in isolation but the Trinity-God and, in particular, God the Father. The encyclical begins by saying, "It is 'God, who is rich in mercy' [Ephesians 2:4] whom Jesus Christ has revealed to us as Father: it is His very Son who, in Himself, has manifested Him and made Him known to us [cf.John 1:18; Hebrews 1:1ff]."[63]

The crucified and risen Jesus, whom we contemplate in the image associated with the feast, is not at the beginning but at the end of the history of divine mercy. He is the historical manifestation of a mercy so deep that its ultimate source is in the Father's heart within the Trinity. In instituting this feast, Pope John Paul II went to the essence of the revelations given to St. Faustina. He identified among the many sayings Jesus addressed to her the one that explains all the others: "I desire the first Sunday after Easter to be the Feast of Mercy. Through the Word Incarnate, I made known the bottomless depth of My Mercy."[64]

The one who speaks this way can only be God the Father! Seen in this light, both the feast and the devotion to divine mercy can be invaluable instruments for evangelization by the Church. They can help us change the erroneous idea of God the Father that is rooted in the human subconscious and is perhaps the principal cause of the rejection of God by nonbelievers.

The Feast of Divine Mercy has a limitation, however: it is a feast without its own liturgy. No one presumed, and rightly so, to change the character and the liturgical content of the first Sunday

---

[63] John Paul II, *Dives in misericordia* [Rich in Mercy], n. 1.
[64] See *Diary of Saint Maria Faustina Kowalska*, 88 (Stockbridge, MA: Marian Press, 2010), p. 44.

that comes after Easter, known since antiquity as "*Dominica in albis depositis.*" There are already readings chronologically linked to the Sunday after Easter, like the appearance of Jesus in the upper room and the episode with Thomas. Rather than constituting a new feast day, the Feast of Divine Mercy adds an extra significance to a particular Sunday of the year, the way the Sunday of the Good Shepherd does.

The actual liturgical feast of Christ's merciful love, however, remains the Solemnity of the Sacred Heart of Jesus, celebrated on the Friday after the Solemnity of the Most Holy Body and Blood of Christ. Since it does not fall on a Sunday, it retains a mystical quality; it is a feast for "intimate friends." The readings for this feast, whether from the Liturgy of the Hours (a passage from St. Bonaventure on the pierced heart of Christ, refuge of beloved souls!) or from the Liturgy of the Eucharist, have been especially well chosen.

We know that in the Bible, the cognitive, volitional, and affective center of a person is the heart. The texts that are most applicable to the tender, merciful love of God in the Old Testament refer to God's heart. As we move from the Old to the New Testament, there is a leap in quality here as well, this time from metaphor to reality. The heart of God was also made flesh!

After the Incarnation, the heart has become a real symbol for us—a symbol and a reality combined—because we know that Christ has a human heart, that there is a human heart that beats within the Trinity. If Christ is indeed risen from the dead, then his heart has risen from the dead as well. It lives, like the rest of his body, in a dimension that is different from before (spiritual, not fleshly), but it lives. If the Lamb is alive in heaven—"a Lamb standing, as though it had been slain" (Revelation 5:6)—then his heart shares in that same state too. It is a pierced heart, but it is alive, eternally pierced because it is eternally alive.

Perhaps this is the certitude that was lacking (or was not sufficiently expressed) in the traditional worship of the Sacred Heart and that can contribute to renewing and revitalizing that worship. The Sacred Heart is not just the heart that beat in Christ's breast when he was on earth and was pierced on the cross and whose presence is perpetuated among us by faith and devotion, especially the Eucharist. That heart lives not only through our devotion but in reality as well; it is not only to be found in the past but also in the present.

In the human body the heart is the engine for everything; if it shuts down, everything shuts down. It takes the blood that carries impurities in the body, purifies it through the lungs, and redistributes it renewed and pure to all the body's members. Well, the heart of Christ does all of this in his mystical body, which is the Church. Ever since Augustine, we say that the Holy Spirit is the soul of the Church,[65] but these two things coincide. The Holy Spirit was in the water and the blood that poured out from Christ's side.

---

[65] See St. Augustine, "Sermon 267," 4, in *Sermons on the Liturgical Seasons 230-272-B*, part 3, vol. 7, *The Works of Saint Augustine*, ed. John E. Rotelle (Hyde Park, NY: New City Press, 1993), 273; see *PL* 38, p. 1231.

Devotion to the Sacred Heart did not complete its task with the disappearance of Jansenism, which was among the reasons for its institution. It is still the best antidote even today for the abstraction, intellectualism, and formalism that withers theology and faith so much. A beating heart is what most clearly distinguishes a living reality from the concept of that reality, a concept that can encompass everything about a person but not that person's beating heart.

3. Renewing the Content of the Feast "in the Spirit"

To release the potential for sanctification and evangelization in these two feasts of mercy, they continually need to be "renewed in the Spirit," to be freed from biased interpretations and even distortions due to our inability to maintain the purity and diversity of the things of God. One antiphon for the Feast of the Sacred Heart, quoting Psalm 33:11, refers to "the thoughts of his heart to all generations." The thoughts of his heart do not change, but generations do!

Two aspects of the feasts of mercy need to be renewed. The first concerns the meaning and the place of the "pious practices" connected to them: the first Fridays of each month for the Feast of the Sacred Heart and the novenas and various chaplets for the Feast of Divine Mercy. If they are not accompanied by solid catechesis, they risk having people believe that the mercy of God is the reward for such pious practices: if you do this and that, you will receive this or that. There is an innate tendency in everyone to want to "give to God the price of his life" (Psalm 49:7), which completely reverses the relationship between faith and works. Pious practices, like all "good works," are righteous and holy if they are seen as a response to grace and not as its cause.

The pious practices mentioned, and others as well, have served and still serve for so many people to express their faith and devotion; they cannot therefore easily be tossed aside. They need instead to be put back patiently in their right place, with an explanation that the mercy of God is always without conditions, even if it is never without consequences. The tacit assumption, however, should never be, "If you say these prayers the right number of times and in the right way, God will give you forgiveness, leniency, immediate entrance into heaven, and so on." Instead, the presupposition should be, "God has given you forgiveness and mercy; thank him, praise him, and bless him for it. Do what the Church prays in the 'Gloria': 'We praise you, we bless you, we adore you, we glorify you, we give you thanks for your great glory.'" God does not practice the rule of *do ut des* with us—"I give so that you will give"; much less can we practice it with him. With God we can only practice the religion of *do quia dedisti*—"I give because I have received, because you have given to me."

The second pitfall to avoid with these feasts and every celebration of divine mercy concerns the precise content to ascribe to this phrase. God's mercy, as we have seen, is not only *agape* but *eros* as well! It is not only forgiveness of sins but also tenderness and visceral love; in the prophets and in the Song of Songs, we see an impassioned, jealous love. In other words, God is not just performing charity toward us; he loves us, he desires us. He seems unable to be happy without us. This is how he wants our love for him to be as well.

We cannot love God with a merciful love when mercy is understood only as forgiveness. (Can we forgive God for something?) We can, however, love him with a merciful love in the sense of a heartfelt, visceral love that can move us to the point of tears—a love of heartfelt gratitude.

May the feasts of mercy serve to make us remember all of this.

CHAPTER 15

"Blessed are the merciful, for they shall obtain mercy" FROM GIFT TO DUTY

We have now come to the point at which we need to move from the mercy of God and Christ to our mercy, to move from gift to duty. Christianity, unlike every other religion or religious philosophy, does not begin by telling people what they need to do to be saved; it begins by telling people what God has done to save them. It does not begin with the duty but with the gift. Duties and commandments—and more exacting than ever—are involved, but they rank second, not first. Before the duty comes the gift; before works, grace.

The clearest example concerns the first and greatest law to love God, and then to love our neighbor (see Luke 10:27). We are not the ones who loved God first, St. John asserts. God was the one who first loved us; we love because he loved us (see 1 John 4:10, 19). This, we will see, is the case with regard to mercy as well. The Latin word for mercy, "*misericordia*," comes from two words, "*misereor*" and "*cor*." They mean "to have pity in our hearts, "to be moved," in regard to the suffering or the mistakes of our brothers and sisters. This is the way that God, as we have seen, describes his mercy when his people stray: "My heart recoils within me, / my compassion grows warm and tender" (Hosea 11:8).

1. Our Mercy: Cause or Effect of God's Mercy?

Jesus says, "Blessed are the merciful, for they shall obtain mercy" (Matthew 5:7), and in the Lord's Prayer he tells us to pray, "Forgive us our trespasses, as we forgive those who trespass against us." He also says, "If you do not forgive men their trespasses, neither will your Father forgive your trespasses" (6:15). These statements could lead us to believe that God's mercy toward us is the result of our mercy toward others and is proportionate to it. If this were the case, however, the relationship between grace and good works would be completely turned upside down, and it would cancel out the purely gratuitous character of divine mercy that God solemnly proclaimed to Moses: "I will be gracious to whom I will be gracious, and will show mercy on whom I will show mercy" (Exodus 33:19).

We should have mercy, then, *because* we have received mercy and not *in order to* receive mercy. We need to have mercy for others since otherwise the mercy of God will not be effective for us and will be withdrawn. Grace always "comes first" and is what creates our obligation to respond: "As the Lord has forgiven you, so you also must forgive," Paul writes to the Colossians (3:13). If the beatitude about the merciful God's mercy toward us seems to be the result of our mercy toward our brothers and sisters, it is because Jesus is speaking there about mercy from the perspective of the final judgment ("they shall obtain mercy" in the future!). St. James writes, in fact, that "judgment is without mercy to one who has shown no mercy; yet mercy triumphs over judgment" (2:13).

The parable of the unmerciful servant (Matthew 18:23-34) is the key to correctly interpreting the relationship between God's mercy and our mercy. We see there how the master, taking the initiative, unconditionally forgives his servant an immense debt (10,000 talents!). And it was precisely his generosity that should have moved this servant to have pity on the one who owed him the paltry sum of 100 denarii.

The king in the parable obviously represents God, and the servants represent human beings. They owe him everything; they need to receive everything from him. But God does not demand any rights for himself; he asks nothing from people that can be of any profit for himself. His mercy is a freely given gift, in superabundance, without any conditions beforehand. Although this love is radically without conditions, it is not without consequences. God wants people not only to accept this gratuitous love that he first gives them without measure but also to allow this love to live in them and permeate their whole being. And this is precisely what the first servant in the parable refuses to do. He accepts the benefit of the master's infinite gift, of course, but he intends to keep it for himself, to lock it up inside himself. He is blocking the free flowing of love.

2. Being Merciful like the Heavenly Father

Why has God established such a close connection between his mercy toward us and our mercy toward one another? Jesus says to his disciples, "Love one another; even as I have loved you, that you also love one another" (John 13:34), and John asserts, "Beloved, if God so loved us, we also ought to love one another" (1 John 4:11). (He does not say, "We also ought to love him back"!) One might say that God is almost more concerned about our love for our neighbor than about our love for him. Here we experience firsthand the difference between human love that flows through a closed circuit and God's love that flows through an open circuit. The character Violetta in *La Traviata* by Giuseppe Verdi sings, "Love me, Alfredo, love me as I love you." The rule here is "I love you, so love me back"; with God, the rule is "I love you, so love your brother."

Why this shift from love for God to love for neighbor? The most direct answer is that we are still living in the flesh, so everything has to happen through the flesh. Even love has to incarnate itself in order to be authentic and not be disembodied, fading away into nothing. Since we are not able, then, to love God in this concrete, practical way with both soul and body because we cannot see him, we are directed to the neighbor whom we do see (see 1 John 4:20). Our neighbor, the other, is the visible face of God for me.

St. Catherine of Siena clarifies another equally fundamental reason for this change of trajectory. She reports God saying to her,

> I require that you should love Me with the same love with which I love. This indeed you cannot do, because I loved you without being loved. All the love which you have for Me you owe to Me, so that it is not of grace that you love Me, but because you ought to do so. . . . I love you of grace and not because I owe you My love. Therefore to Me, in person, you cannot repay the love which I require of you, and I have placed you in the midst of your fellows, that you may do to them that which you cannot do to Me, that is to say, that you may love your neighbor of free grace without expecting any return from him, and what you do to him, I count as done to Me.[66]

It is clear that we sinful human beings cannot love God with a "merciful" love; we cannot have mercy on God. Therefore, that merciful love is given to our neighbor. It allows us to realize the seemingly impossible command from Jesus to "Be merciful, even as your Father is merciful" (Luke 6:36). It allows us to do for others exactly what God does for us. And God considers it—another feature of his infinite mercy!—as if we did it to him personally: "You did it to me!" (Matthew 25:40).

---

[66] Catherine of Siena, *The Dialogue of St. Catherine of Siena*, 64, ed. Paul A. Boer Sr. (N.P.: *Veritatis Splendor*, 2012), p. 81.

Mercy toward our neighbors, unlike God's mercy toward us, is not, however, a *gift* we give them but a *duty* we owe them: "Owe no one anything, except to love one another" (Romans 13:8). Why is it a debt? We have received an infinite measure of love to share with our brothers and sisters. However much we love a brother or sister, we can never match the measure of mercy for them that we have received from God and that is owed to them. God had infinite mercy toward us in giving us his Son Jesus, and he asks us not to keep him just for ourselves but to share him. He asks that the water he has given us become in us "a spring of water welling up to eternal life" (John 4:14). Brothers and sisters who knock at your door are thus creditors who are collecting their debt. Even if you cannot always give them what they ask you for, see that you do not send them away without what is owed to them.

We can see from all this that the essential reason for loving our neighbors is not extrinsic to us but intrinsic: it is not because God commands us to love them, nor is it because they are loved by God and therefore worthy of being loved by us. It is because God has placed in us, has entrusted to us, his own love for them. This is fundamentally the theological virtue of charity insofar as it is an infused virtue; it is a participation in the very love of God. It makes us become participants in the divine nature, which is love, and thus we have a new capacity to love like God loves.

3. Mercy, a Meeting Ground for Religions

Mercy is perhaps the clearest intersection point between Christianity and Buddhism. In Buddhism compassion for every living being constitutes "righteous action" and is one of the steps in the "Noble Eightfold Path" that brings a person to illumination. The motivation is different in these two religious worlds, however. In Christianity the basis is that the human being is created in the image of a God who is "the Father of mercies and God of all comfort" (2 Corinthians 1:3), a God who "lovest all things that exist, / and hast loathing for none of the things which thou hast made" (Wisdom 11:24).

The basis in Buddhism, which does not acknowledge the idea of a personal God and creator, is anthropological and cosmic: human beings should be merciful because of the solidarity and the responsibility that links them to all living things. This difference, however, should not prevent us from working together on a practical level, especially today when life is so threatened with violence and when relationships have become so bitter and "merciless." We Christians can learn much from the books of the current Dalai Lama, Tenzin Gyatso, that propose an "ethic of peace and compassion" for the third millennium.[67] On every page his books exude a great sense of solidarity and almost of tenderness toward

---

[67] See, for example, Dalai Lama, Tenzin Gyatso, *Ethics for a New Millennium* (New York: Riverhead Books, 1999), passim.

all living things and suggest how to transfer this vision into politics, economics, and all other areas of life.

While mercy as an attitude and as a human virtue brings Christianity and Buddhism together in some way, mercy as an attribute of God brings us close to Judaism and Islam, the two other great monotheistic religions. Pope Francis himself has highlighted this in his Bull for the Jubilee Year when he writes,

> There is an aspect of mercy that goes beyond the confines of the Church. It relates us to Judaism and Islam, both of which consider mercy to be one of God's most important attributes. Israel was the first to receive this revelation which continues in history as the source of an inexhaustible richness meant to be shared with all mankind. . . . Among the privileged names that Islam attributes to the Creator are "Merciful and Kind." This invocation is often on the lips of faithful Muslims who feel themselves accompanied and sustained by mercy in their daily weakness. They too believe that no one can place a limit on divine mercy because its doors are always open.[68]

4. The Oil That Runs Down Aaron's Beard

Augustine says, "We are mortal human beings, fragile, weak, carrying along with us our earthen vessels, which don't leave each other

---

[68] Pope Francis, *Misericordiae vultus*, n. 23. On the topic of mercy in the interreligious dialogue, see Walter Kasper, *Mercy: The Essence of the Gospel and the Key to Christian Life* (Mahwah, NJ: Paulist Press, 2014).

much room."[69] We cannot live together in harmony, in a family or any other kind of community, without the reciprocal practice of forgiveness and mercy. We need to respond with forgiveness and even, as far as possible, by excusing others instead of condemning them. The following saying applies to us: "He who excuses himself, God accuses him; he who accuses himself, God excuses him." In terms of others, the converse applies: "He who excuses his brother is excused by God; he who accuses his brother is accused by God."

Forgiveness does for a community what oil does for a motor. If someone begins a trip in a car without a drop of oil in the engine, after a few minutes the whole car will be on fire. Like oil, forgiveness neutralizes friction. Having mercy for one another should be the most natural sentiment for human beings. We would have to close our ears and our eyes to the cry of desolation that reaches us from all sides not to have at least some compassion.

I have used the image of oil. There is a psalm that sings of the goodness and joy of living together in harmony, which says it is "like the precious oil upon the head" that runs down Aaron's beard and robes (see Psalm 133:2). Our Aaron, our high priest, is Christ; mercy and forgiveness comprise the oil that runs down his "head" lifted up on the cross and that spreads down through the body of the Church to the hem of its garments, to those who live at its margins.

---

[69] St. Augustine, "Sermon 69," 1, trans. Edmund Hill, part 3, vol. 3, *The Works of Saint Augustine*, ed. John E. Rotelle (Brooklyn: New City, 1991), p. 235; see *PL* 38, p. 441.

On a practical level, let us try to identify among our relationships the one that seems to us most in need of having the oil of mercy and reconciliation, and let us quietly pour oil on that relationship in abundance. The psalm concludes by saying that wherever people live in forgiveness and reciprocal mercy, "there the LORD has commanded the blessing, / life for evermore" (Psalm 133:3).

CHAPTER 16

Put on Visceral Mercy
BENEVOLENCE BEFORE BENEFICENCE

1. Works of Mercy and Visceral Mercy

Having mercy does not mean just forgiving our neighbor. The Church encourages us to engage in the seven so-called works of corporal mercy: feeding the hungry, giving drink to the thirsty, clothing the naked, welcoming strangers, visiting the sick, visiting those in prison, and burying the dead. The first six are mentioned by Jesus in Matthew 25, while the seventh is inspired by the Book of Tobit (see 2:3-7). Alongside these works of corporal mercy, the *Catechism* also includes the "spiritual works of mercy": counseling the doubtful, instructing the ignorant, admonishing sinners, comforting the sorrowful, forgiving all injuries, forbearing troublesome people patiently, and praying for the living and the dead.[70]

As always, these lists are suggestive rather than exhaustive. Furthermore, they need to be updated and adapted to the times and to the new situations of corporal and spiritual suffering of humanity. For example, we should add "not abandoning the elderly" to the list of corporal works of mercy and "forming one's children in the faith" to the spiritual works of mercy.

---

[70] See *Catechism of the Catholic Church*, 2447.

But I do not want to reflect so much on the "works" of mercy in this chapter as on the "viscera" of mercy—not on the mercy of hands, but on the mercy of the heart—in other words, on the sentiments and inner dispositions that should accompany "acts" of mercy. St. Paul wrote to the Colossians, "Put on . . . compassion [visceral mercy], kindness, lowliness, meekness, and patience, forbearing one another and, if one has a complaint against another, forgiving each other" (3:12-13).

The word "compassion" is a translation that is toned down from the much stronger and more realistic expression in the original text that speaks about "the viscera, or bowels, of compassion" (*splangna oiktirmou*). That image, as we have seen, is used elsewhere in the Bible to describe God's mercy; therefore, it is as if the apostle was saying, "Be merciful as God is merciful, not just in doing good, but in having goodwill toward others."

This Pauline insight about mercy reveals, beyond the visible world of charity comprised of words and deeds, another completely inner world that, in relationship to the first one, is like what the soul is to the body. *Doing* good, the works of mercy, needs to originate from *desiring* the good for others. Benevolence comes before beneficence, goodwill before charity.

The apostle says, "Let love be genuine" (Romans 12:9). The original word used by St. Paul and translated as "genuine" is *anhypokritos*, meaning "without hypocrisy." This word is a kind of "indicator light"; it is actually a rare term in the New Testament, which we find used almost exclusively to define Christian love.

That word appears again in 2 Corinthians 6:6, as well as in 1 Peter 1:22 where it is translated there as "sincere." The text from Peter, in particular, allows us to understand the meaning of the word in question very clearly because he explains it with another phrase: "sincere love," he says, consists in loving one another "earnestly from the heart."

Paul specifies the difference between the two types of charity, saying that the greatest act of visible mercy—giving all of one's goods to the poor—amounts to nothing without an inner attitude of charity (see 1 Corinthians 13:3). This would be the opposite of "sincere" charity. Hypocritical charity is charity that does good but without the inner disposition of goodwill; it is an outward, visible charity that does not reflect the heart. In this case, people seem to be doing charitable works, but those works can be based, at worst, in self-centeredness, a search for oneself, the exploitation of a brother or sister, or even simply a remorseful conscience.

It would be a fatal mistake, of course, to set the mercy of the heart in opposition to the works of mercy or to hide behind heart-felt mercy as an excuse for not doing any actual works of charity. The issue here is not to diminish the importance of the works of mercy as much as it is to ensure a secure basis for them against selfishness and endless dissimulation.

Mercy of the heart is what shines through in Jesus' actions. Before reporting a healing or a miracle by Jesus, the Gospels almost always speak about his being moved and feeling compassion. In answer to a leper asking Jesus if he would heal him, Mark writes,

"Moved with pity, he stretched out his hand and touched him, and said to him, 'I will; be clean'" (1:41). Seeing the sorrow of the widow of Nain, Jesus "had compassion on her" (Luke 7:13)—literally, "his viscera, his bowels, were moved"! The same thing occurs before he multiplies the loaves of bread (see Matthew 15:32) and in many other cases. Here too, Jesus is visibly demonstrating the sentiments of the heavenly Father toward human beings. The father in the parable, seeing his prodigal son return, "had compassion" (Luke 15:20)—again a translation that is toned down from the original that says, "his viscera were moved (*esplangnisthe*)."

The English phrase that best translates this biblical metaphor is the phrase "deep, heartfelt emotion." This phrase needs to be rescued from a superficial and sometimes negative connotation, as if it were something that strong people should be ashamed of. When it is sincere and comes from the heart, deep emotion is the most eloquent response that is worthiest of human beings in the face of a great love or a great sorrow. In every case, heartfelt emotion benefits whoever receives it. No word or gesture or gift can substitute for it because it is the best gift. It means opening oneself up to the other. For that reason, modesty accompanies it, just as it does for the most intimate and sacred things people experience, when they no longer belong completely to themselves but to another. Compassionate emotion cannot be entirely suppressed without depriving others of something that belongs to them, because it has sprung up on their behalf.

2. Mercy in Judgments

In his papal bull for the Year of Jubilee, Pope Francis emphasizes an area in which it is important to practice mercy of the heart: the area of judgments. He writes, "If anyone wishes to avoid God's judgment, he should not make himself the judge of his brother or sister. Human beings, whenever they judge, look no farther than the surface, whereas the Father looks into the very depths of the soul."[71]

Jesus says, "Judge not, that you be not judged. . . . Why do you see the speck that is in your brother's eye, but do not notice the log that is in your own eye?" (Matthew 7:1, 3). Jesus does not mean, "Do not judge people and they will not judge you," because we know from experience that things do not always work this way. Instead, he means, "Do not judge your brother or sister so that God will not judge you." Or, even better, "Do not judge your brother or sister because God has not judged you." The Lord compares the neighbor's sin (the sin that is judged!) to a speck, no matter what it is, in contrast to the sin of those who judge (the sin of judging) that he calls a log. The log is the very fact of judging; that is how serious it is in God's eyes.

Any discussion about judgments is nuanced and complicated, so if the topic is only partially covered, it will immediately seem unrealistic. How can we actually live our lives without judging?

---

[71] *Misericordiae vultus*, n. 14.

Our judgment is implicit even in a look. We cannot observe, listen, and live without evaluating things, without judging things. It is not so much judgment that we need to remove from our hearts as it is the venom, the malice, the condemnation in our judgment! In Luke's compilation of Jesus' sayings, Jesus' command "Judge not, and you will not be judged" is immediately clarified in the very same verse by the command that comes next: "Condemn not, and you will not be condemned" (Luke 6:37).

In itself, judging is a neutral action; a judgment can end in condemnation or in acquittal and justification. Negative judgments are the ones being referred to and banned by the word of God, the ones that condemn the sinner as well as the sin. A mother and an outsider can judge the imperfection a baby objectively has, but how different their two judgments are! The mother actually suffers over this imperfection as if it were hers; she feels herself jointly responsible and is determined to help get it corrected. She does not go around shouting from the rooftops that her baby has an imperfection. Well, our judgment of a brother or a sister should be similar to that of the mother because "we, though many, are . . . individually members one of another" (Romans 12:5). These others are part of "our own family."

3. Mercy in a Person's Gaze

One thing that clearly emerges in reading the Gospels is the importance of Jesus' eyes, his gaze. Many encounters with him are initiated and determined by a look of love and mercy on his part. This is the case with the rich young man (see Mark 10:21), with Zacchaeus (see Luke 19:5), and with Peter after his betrayal (see Luke 22:61). His gaze was not a hasty gaze; at times the Gospel says, "He looked around" (see Mark 3:34). Neither was it a superficial gaze but one that reached people in their innermost beings. He "sees the heart" (see Luke 16:15). His gaze is always one of mercy and acceptance when he is with people who are open or searching, but when he is with hypocrites or hostile people, it can be terrible: "He looked around at them with anger" (Mark 3:5).

It has been said that many things have changed down through the centuries, but the language of the eyes has not changed: a smile, tears, fear, wonder, and trust are the same everywhere. Jesus said, "The eye is the lamp of the body. So, if your eye is sound, your whole body will be full of light" (Matthew 6:22). The eyes are the mirror of the soul. Looking into people's eyes is like knocking at their door. When someone knocks on our door, we can react in many ways: we can decide not to respond and just look through the peephole; we can keep the door ajar without quite letting them in. Sentiments are clearly reflected in the eyes of people when they meet each other, whether it be fear, indifference, and weariness . . . or joy, satisfaction, enthusiasm, and availability. How sad that some eyes do not let light in or show their feelings; they are like boarded-up windows.

Modern medicine has been able to diagnose sicknesses by looking into a person's eye. So too illnesses of the soul are instantly reflected in people's eyes. The eyes of insecure people never look directly at someone and never sustain the gaze of another person for long; the eyes of arrogant and presumptuous people always create a distance between themselves and others; the eyes of vain people only see themselves even when they are looking at others; the eyes of egotists see others from the perspective of possible advantages to themselves; the eyes of deceivers try to find the weak point of other people to "sell their wares"; the eyes of sensual people never see other people as human beings but only as objects to gratify their desires.

I say all this to make the point that we all have a valuable means at our disposal to exercise mercy: our gaze. It can be like balm for a wound or, unfortunately, like vinegar on a sore. What St. James says about the tongue (3:5-10) can also be said about eyes. We can kill with our eyes or bring life, spew venom or comfort someone's heart.

4. Mercy, a Virtue for Someone with Nothing to Give

Mercy in one's gaze is a mercy that everyone can and should exercise. Søren Kierkegaard, in addition to being a philosopher, was also a great believer and a friend of Jesus. He has some wonderful insights on mercy as the virtue above all of a person who has nothing to give except a gaze of mercy. He writes, "One can be merciful without having the least thing to give. This is of great importance, since *being able* to be merciful certainly is a far greater perfection than to have money and then *to be able* to give. . . . Have merci-fulness; then money can be given—without it money smells bad [italics original]."[72]

We do immense injury to people who are poor if we consider them only as objects and as recipients of mercy, as those who at best should bow and scrape in gratitude whenever the rich deign to have mercy. Kierkegaard exclaims, "What mercilessness!" it is to think of the poor as being unable to be merciful themselves.[73] Let us listen to the philosopher as he imagines addressing a hypo-thetical poor person:

> One can be merciful . . . to the highest degree . . . in the eminent and excellent sense when one has nothing to give. . . . Be mer-ciful, be merciful toward the rich! Remember what you have in your power, while he has the money! Do not misuse this power; do not be so merciless as to call down heaven's punishment upon his mercilessness! . . . If the rich person is stingy and close-fisted, or even if he is close-fisted not only with money but just as stingy with words and [is] repelling—then you be rich in mercifulness! . . . Mercifulness is *how* it is given. . . . I can perceive mercifulness in the pennies [of the poor widow] just as well as in the hundred thousand [of the rich man].[74]

---

[72] Søren Kierkegaard, *Works of Love*, trans. and ed. Henry V. Wong and Edna H. Wong (Princeton, NJ: Princeton University Press, 1995), pp. 317, 321.
[73] Ibid., p. 322.
[74] Ibid., pp. 322–323, 327.

This is what Jesus wanted to teach his disciples when the poor widow put in two coins in the Temple treasury; he said she had given more than all the rich donors (see Mark 12:42-43). Mercy, fortunately for us, does not discriminate between rich and poor, between the haves and the have-nots. It is a virtue for everyone and, as the philosopher reminded us, a virtue above all for those who have nothing to give.

CHAPTER 17

The Mercy of Outsiders
THE PARABLE OF THE GOOD SAMARITAN

1. Mercy and the Law

In music and in world literature, there are some "openings" that have become famous. When four notes, for example, are arranged in a certain sequence, every listener immediately exclaims, "Beethoven's Fifth Symphony, 'Fate knocking at the door.'" Those four notes are a kind of signature, an unmistakable trademark. Many of Jesus' parables share this characteristic of famous beginnings. One of them is the one I will comment on now. When a Christian hears, "A man was going down from Jerusalem to Jericho" (Luke 10:30), he or she will say, "The parable of the Good Samaritan!"

Let us reread it in the context of what Jesus wanted to teach about mercy: first, the law needs to yield to mercy at times; second, mercy, before being a Christian virtue, is a requirement and a virtue that is feasible for all human beings and is practiced outside of Christianity. Let us see what circumstance instigated the parable:

And behold, a lawyer stood up to put him to the test, saying, "Teacher, what shall I do to inherit eternal life?" He said to him, "What is written in the law? How do you read?" And he answered, "You shall love the Lord your God with all your heart, and with all your soul, and with all your strength, and with all your mind; and your neighbor as yourself." And he said to him, "You have answered right; do this, and you will live." But he, desiring to justify himself, said to Jesus, "And who is my neighbor?" (Luke 10:25-29)

This is yet another attempt to catch Jesus in a trap. The lawyer demonstrates that he knows very well what to do to receive eternal life. He asks the question to force Jesus to compromise himself. If he gives the standard response that everyone already knows, he is bringing nothing new to the Mosaic law and does not deserve his fame. If he responds in another way, he can be accused of being a heretic. Jesus answers the lawyer's question with a problem, or better, with an example:

Jesus replied, "A man was going down from Jerusalem to Jericho, and he fell among robbers, who stripped him and beat him, and departed, leaving him half dead. Now by chance a priest was going down that road; and when he saw him he passed by on the other side. So likewise a Levite, when he came to the place and saw him, passed by on the other side. But a Samaritan, as he journeyed, came to where he was; and when he saw him, he had compassion, and went to him and bound up his wounds, pouring on oil and wine; then he set him on his own beast and brought him to an inn, and took care of him. And the next day he took out two denarii and gave them to the innkeeper, saying, 'Take care of him; and whatever more you spend, I will repay you when I come back.' Which of these three, do you think, proved neighbor to the man who fell among the robbers?" He said, "The one who showed mercy on him." And Jesus said to him, "Go and do likewise." (Luke 10:30-37)

Note that the Samaritan's work of mercy also came from "visceral" mercy: "he had compassion," a phrase that is the typical euphemism for "his viscera were moved." The feature most often highlighted from this parable is the total reversal of the traditional concept of a neighbor. The neighbor turns out to be the good Samaritan rather than the wounded man as we would have expected. This means that we do not need to wait passively for a neighbor to pop up suddenly on our street. It is up to us to be aware of what is happening around us and be ready to notice things. The neighbor is who each of us is called to become! The lawyer's problem seems to be turned upside down; an abstract, academic issue becomes a concrete, practical issue. The question to ask is not, "Who is my neighbor?" but "For whom can I be a neighbor here and now?"

Jesus implicitly also answers the question about how to be a neighbor: with actions and not just words. John says, "Little children, let us not love in word or speech but in deed and in truth" (1 John 3:18). If the good Samaritan had been satisfied to approach the unfortunate man lying in a pool of his own blood and say, "Poor fellow. I am so sorry! How did this happen? Hang in there!" or similar words and then went on his way, wouldn't that have been an irony and an affront?

This is the general teaching of the parable, but it is not the only one. No less important is the teaching it gives about the relationship between the law and mercy. The startling fact is that the priest and the Levite *needed* to act as they did according to the law. The wounded man to all appearances was dead, and Mosaic law forbad priests to touch a dead body lest they become unclean and then unable to exercise their priestly ministry (see Leviticus 21:1). What they did not understand is that although the law is righteous and necessary, because every society needs to have rules, there are cases in which people should go beyond the law.[75] At times, as is the case here, *summum jus, summa injuria*, a law taken to its extreme becomes unjust. True righteousness in this case is not to observe the law but to break it. This is the point that Jesus was trying to make to those who opposed him about his healings on the Sabbath: the law about Sabbath rest is sacrosanct, but it is "for the sake of the people" and should be broken when a person's very life hangs in the balance.

---

[75] See Alphonse Maillot, *Le parabole di Gesù* (Cinisello Balsamo: Edizioni San Paolo, 1997), pp. 112–114.

2. A Samaritan!

This is not the first time Jesus proposes a Samaritan as an example to be imitated; that is, someone who, because of his ethnic group, was considered by the Jews to be a heretic and or a foreigner. But in this case, that detail takes on an important significance for us. It means mercy is not the exclusive prerogative of Christians, and at times the action of outsiders can be an example for us to put people's needs ahead of ecclesiastical rules.

By choosing a Samaritan as the hero of the story, Jesus is telling us that people do not need to share the same faith and the same religious convictions to exercise mercy. Mercy has a basis and a justification that are prior to faith but that faith promotes and does not disregard: the sentiment of solidarity with humanity. This allows us to be glad about and to admire the mercy practiced outside the Church by secular institutes like the Red Cross, Doctors without Borders, and many others. In Matthew 25, Jesus did not seem to make distinctions between those who did works of mercy in his name and those who simply fed the hungry and cared for the sick. He said about all of them, "You did it to me!" (Matthew 25:40).

The parable of the Good Samaritan has a new area of application in our own time that is close to the literal aspect of the story. We are having a problem with contemporary "robbers" who leave people half-dead in the streets. These hit-and-run drivers, the so-called pirates of the street, are irresponsible and aggressive drivers who cause tragedy in our streets daily, and such accidents are often fatal. The priest and the Levite are those who, in such cases, do not help out because they want to avoid any trouble and not get their hands dirty or lose time. Good Samaritans, besides those who stop to lend assistance to the victims of these accidents, are all those who work to make our streets safer: people in charge of traffic control and roadside assistance and police officers on the street. We owe all of them gratitude, even if we have to pay some well-deserved fines for moving violations at times.

3. A Planet under Attack by Predators

Pope Francis's encyclical on the environment, *Laudato si'*, prompts me to one further application of the parable of the Good Samaritan. It was certainly not Jesus' intention at the moment he told it, but it is the nature of his words to be "open structures" capable of taking on new meanings and having new applications due to changing times and situations. Pope Francis writes, "The violence present in our hearts, wounded by sin, is also reflected in the symptoms of sickness evident in the soil, in the water, in the air and in all forms of life. This is why the earth herself, burdened and laid waste, is among the most abandoned and maltreated of our poor; she groans in travail (Romans 8:22)."[76]

---

[76] Pope Francis, *Laudato si'*, n. 2.

St. Francis of Assisi, who inspired the encyclical,[77] had already given a human face to creation, making every creature a brother or a sister: Brother Sun, Sister Moon, Mother Earth, and so on. It is true that the earth today resembles the unfortunate man assaulted by robbers and left for dead in the street. It has been ravaged, severely wounded, and stripped of its most precious goods: water, plants, species of animals and vegetation that are in danger of extinction. Many pass by and go on their way, pretending they do not see, or simply leave it to others to take concern for the problem later in the future.

If this be the case, the pope, by courageously denouncing it, has shown himself to be "the Good Samaritan" for our "Sister, Mother Earth." With the space he dedicated in his encyclical to the contribution of science and various human institutions (both religious and secular) that have been dealing with the problem, he is recognizing, in the wake of Jesus, the contribution of "outsiders" to the common problems of humanity. They are merciful without knowing it, which is the best way for us to be merciful as well.

---

[77] *Laudato si'* ["Be praised"] is a repeated phrase in the famous prayer by St. Francis that praises God for his creation. The prayer's title in English is "Canticle of the Sun" or "Canticle of Creatures."

CHAPTER 18

"The Father will give you another counselor"
THE HOLY SPIRIT AND DIVINE MERCY

1. A Year of the Lord's Mercy

Returning to his home in Nazareth after his baptism in the Jordan, Jesus solemnly applies the words of Isaiah to himself:

> "The Spirit of the Lord is upon me,
>
> because he has anointed me to preach good news to the poor.
>
> He has sent me to proclaim release to the captives
>
> and recovering of sight to the blind,
>
> to set at liberty those who are oppressed,
>
> to proclaim the acceptable year of the Lord." (Luke 4:18-19)

It was thanks to the anointing of the Holy Spirit that Jesus preached the good news, healed the sick, comforted the afflicted, and performed all his works of mercy. St. Basil writes that the Holy Spirit was "inseparably present" with Jesus so that his "every operation was wrought with the co-operation of the Spirit."[78] The Holy Spirit, who is love personified in the Trinity, is also the mercy of God personified. He is the very "content" of divine mercy. Without the Holy Spirit, "mercy" would be an empty word.

The name "Paraclete" clearly indicates this. In announcing his coming, Jesus says, "And I will pray the Father, and he will give you another Counselor, to be with you for ever" (John 14:16). "Another" here implies "after having given me, Jesus, to you." The Holy Spirit is, therefore, the one through whom the risen Jesus now continues his work of "doing good and healing all" (Acts 10:38). The statement that the Paraclete "will take what is mine and declare it to you" (John 16:14) also applies to mercy: the Holy Spirit will open the treasures of Jesus' mercy to believers in every age. He will make Jesus' mercy not just be remembered but also experienced.

The Paraclete is active above all in the sacrament of mercy, Confession. "He is the remission of all sins," says one of the Church's prayers.[79] Because of that, before giving absolution to a penitent, a confessor says, "God, the Father of mercies, through the death and resurrection of his Son, has reconciled the world to himself and sent the Holy Spirit among us for the forgiveness of sins; through the ministry of the Church may God give you pardon and peace."

---

[78] St. Basil, *On the Holy Spirit*, XVI, 39, in *Letters and Select Works*, trans. Blomfield Jackson, vol. 8, *Nicene and Post-Nicene Fathers* (repr., Grand Rapids, MI: Eerdmans, 1996), p. 25; see *PG* 32, p. 140.
[79] Roman Missal, Tuesday after Pentecost.

Some Church Fathers considered the oil the Samaritan poured on the wounds of the man who was robbed to be a symbol of the Holy Spirit.[80] A beautiful African-American spiritual expresses this thought with the evocative image of the balm in Gilead: "There is a balm in Gilead, / to heal the sin-sick soul /. . . . / to make the wounded whole." Gilead is a place mentioned in the Old Testament that was famous for its perfumed healing ointment (see Jeremiah 8:22). Listening to this song we could almost imagine a street vendor shouting out a list of his merchandise and their prices. The whole Church should be this "street vendor." The balm the Church offers today is no longer the medicinal ointment of Gilead; it is the Holy Spirit.

2. The Letter and the Spirit, Justice and Mercy

The Holy Spirit is the key to solving the very tricky problem of the relationship between the law and mercy. Commenting on Paul's saying that the letter kills but the Spirit gives life (2 Corinthians 3:3-6), St. Thomas Aquinas writes, "The 'letter' refers to every written law that exists outside of man, including the moral precepts of the gospel. The 'letter' of the gospel, even of its precepts, also kills without the inward presence of the grace of faith that heals us."[81] Shortly before that statement, the holy doctor explains

---

[80] Origen, *Homilies on Luke*, 34, trans. Joseph T. Lienhard, vol. 94, Fathers of the Church (Washington, DC: Catholic University of America Press, 1996), pp. 139-140; see *SCh* 87, p. 401.
[81] St. Thomas Aquinas, *Summa theologiae*, I–IIae, q. 106, a. 2.

what he means by "the grace of faith": "The new law is primarily the same grace of the Holy Spirit that is given to believers."[82]

This is a bold assertion that none of us would dare make if it did not come from two very great doctors of the Latin Church, Augustine and Thomas Aquinas. It finds confirmation earlier in the very words of Christ and the experience of the apostles. If a proclamation of the beatitudes and the moral teachings of the gospel were enough for us to have eternal life, then there would have been no need for Jesus to die and be raised for us to receive the gift of the Spirit. That is why he tells the apostles it is good for him to go away so that he can send the Paraclete upon them (see John 16:7). Look at the experience of the apostles: they had listened to all the precepts of the very author of the gospel, but they were not able to put them into practice until the Holy Spirit came down upon them at Pentecost.

The conclusion that emerges from all this is clear: if even the gospel precepts without the Holy Spirit would be "the letter that kills," what can we say about ecclesiastical laws, monastic rules, and the canons in the canon law, including those that regulate marriage? The Spirit does not abolish or bypass the law;[83] he does, however, teach at what point the law should move aside and yield to mercy. Obviously, not every "letter" kills but only the one that

---

[82] Ibid., q. 106, a. 1; see also St. Augustine, *The Spirit and the Letter*, 21, 36, pp. 221–222.

[83] St. Augustine, *The Spirit and the Letter*, 19, 34: "The law was given that grace might be sought; grace was given that the law might be fulfilled" (p. 220).

claims, all by itself and once and for all, to regulate life or even substitute itself for life.

3. The Holy Spirit Reveals the Merciful Father

An essential work of the Holy Spirit with respect to mercy is also that of changing the picture people have in their minds of God after they sin. One of the causes—perhaps the main one—for the alienation of people today from religion and faith is the distorted image they have of God. It is also the cause of a lifeless Christianity that has no enthusiasm or joy and is lived out more as a duty than as a gift, by constraint rather than by attraction.

What is this "preconceived" idea of God in the collective human unconscious that operates automatically (in computer language, we would say "by default")? To find that out, we only need to ask this question: "What ideas, what words, what feelings spontaneously arise for you before you think about it when you come to the words in the Lord's Prayer 'May your will be done'"? In general, people say it with their heads bent down in resignation inwardly, as if preparing themselves for the worst.

People unconsciously link God's will to everything that is unpleasant and painful, to what in one way or another is seen as destroying individual freedom and development. It is as though God were the enemy of every celebration, joy, and pleasure. People do not take into account that in the New Testament, the will of God is called "*eudokia*" (see Ephesians 1:9; Luke 2:14), meaning, "goodwill, kindness." When we pray, "May your will be done," it is really like saying, "Fulfill in me, Father, your plan of love." Mary said her *fiat* with that attitude, and so did Jesus.

God is generally seen as the Supreme Being, the Omnipotent One, the Lord of time and history, as an entity who asserts his power over an individual from the outside. No detail of human life escapes him. The transgression of the law, disobedience to the divine will, inexorably introduces a disorder into the order willed by God from all eternity. As a consequence, his infinite justice requires reparation: a person will need to do something for God so as to reestablish the order that was disturbed in creation, and this reparation will involve a deprivation, a sacrifice. However, since people are never able to be certain that the "satisfaction" is enough, anxiety arises over facing death and judgment. God is a taskmaster who requires being paid back in full!

Of course, these people do not leave out the mercy of God! But for them, mercy functions only to moderate the necessary rigors of justice. It rectifies the situation, but it is an exception, not the rule. In practice, then, they believe God's love and forgiveness depend on the love and forgiveness they have for others: if you forgive whoever offended you, God will be able in turn to forgive you. It leads to a relationship of bargaining with God. Isn't it true that people think they need to accumulate merits to get into heaven? And don't people attribute great significance to their efforts—to the Masses they attend, to the candles they light, and to the novenas they make?

Since all these practices have allowed so many people in the past to demonstrate their love to God, they cannot be thrown out the window but need to be respected. God makes his flowers bloom in all climates and his saints in all seasons. We cannot deny, however, that again there is a risk here of falling into a utilitarian religion of "*do ut des*," "I give so that you can give, so that I can receive." Behind all of this is the presupposition that a relationship with God depends on human beings. People unconsciously presume to "pay God his price" (see Psalm 49:7); they do not want to be debtors but creditors to God.

Where does this twisted idea of God come from? Let us leave aside individual and incidental factors like a bad relationship with one's earthly father, which, in some cases, puts a strain on the relationship with God the Father. The basic reason for this terrible "preconception" about God clearly appears from what we have just said: the law, the commandments. As long as people live under the reign of sin, under the law, God seems to be a severe Master, someone who is opposed to the fulfillment of a person's earthly desires with his mandates of "You should . . . You should not" that comprise the commandments: "You should not covet other's goods, others' spouses," and so on. In this situation, carnal human beings store up bitterness against God deep in their hearts. They see him as an adversary to their happiness, and if it depended on them, they would be very happy if God did not exist.[84]

The first thing the Holy Spirit does when he comes to dwell in us is to reveal a different face of God to us. He shows him to us as an ally, as a friend, as the one who "did not spare his own Son but gave him up for us all" (Romans 8:32). In brief, the Holy Spirit shows us a very tender Father who has given us the law not to stifle our freedom but to protect it. A filial sentiment then arises that makes us spontaneously cry, "*Abba*, Father." It is like saying, "I did not know you, or I knew you only from hearing about you. Now I know you, I know who you are, and I know that you truly wish good for me and that you look upon me with favor!" A son or daughter has now replaced a servant; love has replaced fear. This is what happens on the subjective and existential level when a person is "born anew of the Spirit" (see John 3:5, 7-8).

In addition to the law, there has been another reason in recent times for resentment against God: human suffering, and especially the suffering of the innocent. A nonbeliever has written that human suffering "is the rock of atheism."[85] The dilemma is that either God can overcome evil but does not want to, so he is not a father; or that he wants to overcome evil but he cannot, so he is not

---

[84] See Martin Luther, "Sermon for Pentecost," *The Sermons of Martin Luther*, vol. 3 (Grand Rapids, MI: Baker Book, 2000), pp. 273–287.
[85] The phrase comes from a 1835 drama by the nineteenth-century German author Georg Büchner, *Danton's Death* [*Dantons Tod*], trans. Howard Brenton and Jane Margaret Fry (London: Methuen, 1982), p. 43. In Act 3, a character asks, "Why do I suffer? That is the rock of atheism."

omnipotent. This is a very old objection, but it has become deafening in the wake of the tragedies of World War II. "No one can believe in a God as Father after Auschwitz," someone has written.

I attempted to explain in the first chapter the answer the Holy Spirit has given the Church about this problem, which is that God suffers alongside people. He is not a far-off God who looks with indifference at a person suffering on earth. To the objection above, one can thus respond that God *can* overcome evil but does not *choose* to do it (at least in a general or normal way) so as not to remove people's free will. God *wants* to overcome evil—and he will—but with a new kind of victory, the victory of love in which he takes evil upon himself and converts it to good for all eternity.

It would be a magnificent fruit of the Year of Mercy if it served to restore the true picture of God that Jesus came to earth to reveal to us.

4. Making Ourselves Paracletes

The title "Paraclete" not only speaks about God's mercy toward us but also opens for us a whole new field of acts of mercy for one another. We need, in other words, to become paracletes ourselves! If it is true that the Christian needs to be an *alter Christus*, "another Christ," it is just as true that he or she needs to become "another paraclete."

The love of God has been poured into our hearts through the Holy Spirit (see Romans 5:5), whether it be the love with which

God loves us or the love that has made us in turn capable of loving God and our neighbor. When applied to mercy—which is the form love takes in the face of the suffering and sin of a person who is loved—the following saying from the apostle tells us something very important: the Paraclete not only comforts us; he also comes to comfort others and makes us able to comfort them and be merciful. St. Paul writes, "Blessed be the God and Father of our Lord Jesus Christ, the Father of mercies and God of all *comfort*, who *comforts* us in all our affliction, so that we may be able to *comfort* those who are in any affliction, with the *comfort* with which we ourselves are *comforted* by God [italics added]" (2 Corinthians 1:3-4). The Greek word from which "Paraclete" is derived appears five times in this text, sometimes as a verb and sometimes as a noun. It contains the essential elements for a theology of consolation. Consolation comes from God who is "the Father of all comfort"; he comes to whoever is afflicted. But he does not stop with that person; his ultimate goal is reached when those who have experienced consolation use that experience in turn to comfort others.

But console how? This is the important point. With the very consolation with which we have been consoled by God—a divine, not human, consolation. That does not happen when we are content to repeat empty words about circumstances that leave things the way we found them: "Don't worry; don't get upset; you'll see that everything will turn out for the best!" We need instead to communicate authentic consolation, which comes from "the encouragement of the scriptures [so that] we might have hope" (Romans 15:4). This also explains the miracles that a simple word or gesture in an atmosphere of prayer can accomplish at the bedside of a sick person. God is giving comfort through you.

In a certain sense, the Holy Spirit needs us in order for him to be the "Paraclete." He wants to comfort, defend, and exhort, but he has no mouth, hands, or eyes to "embody" his consolation. Or better, he has our hands, our eyes, our mouths. Just as our soul acts, moves, and smiles through the members of our body, so the Holy Spirit does the same through the members of "his" body, the Church and us. St. Paul recommends to the early Christians, "Therefore encourage one another" (1 Thessalonians 5:11); translated literally the verb here means "make yourselves paracletes for one another." If the consolation and the mercy we receive from the Spirit do not flow from us to others, if we selfishly want to keep it for ourselves, then very soon it stagnates.

Let us ask for grace from Mary, whom Christian devotion honors with two titles that together signify "paraclete": "*Consoler* of the Afflicted" and "*Advocate* for Sinners." She has certainly made herself a "paraclete" for us! A text from the Second Vatican Council says, "The Mother of Jesus shine[s] forth on earth, until the day of the Lord shall come (cf. 2 Peter 3:10), as a sign of sure hope and solace to the people of God during its sojourn on earth."[86]

---

[86] *Lumen gentium*, n. 68.

Conclusion

The World Will Be Saved by Mercy

The words that one of Dostoevsky's favorite characters says in *The Idiot* are well known and often repeated: "Beauty will save the world." But he immediately follows this with a question: "What kind of beauty will save the world?"[87] It is clear even to Dostoevsky that not every kind of beauty will save the world; there is a beauty that can save the world and a beauty that can devastate the world. Therefore, his conclusion is that "There's only one positively beautiful person in the world—Christ, so that the appearance of this measureless, infinitely beautiful person is in fact . . . of course . . . an infinite miracle."[88] The beauty of Christ is his mercy, and that is what will save the world—not the love of beauty, but the beauty of love.

James writes, "Mercy triumphs over judgment" (2:13). He is probably talking about the mercy practiced by human beings, but the statement is true to a much greater extent if it is applied to God's mercy. It will be God's mercy in the end that will triumph over all injustices and the lack of human mercy. The author of the life of Silvanus of Mount Athos narrates a rather significant episode about a holy monk. This monk, a great man of God, had

[87] Fyodor Dostoevsky, *The Idiot*, III, 5, trans. Henry and Olga Carlisle (New York: New American Library, 1969), p. 402.

[88] Dostoevsky, "Letter to his niece Sonja Ivanova," January 13, 1868, trans. David A. Love, in *Dostoevsky's The Idiot: A Critical Companion*, ed. Liza Knapp (Evanston, IL: Northwestern University Press, 1998), 242–243.

attained such a compassion for humanity that he was always weeping and imploring God's mercy for himself and everyone else. One day when he was close to despair, the Lord appeared to him and asked, "Why are you weeping like this? Do you not know that I am the one who will judge the world? I will have mercy on every person who called on God even once in his life."[89]

Orthodox monastic spirituality is replete with examples of men like this monk, men who had became completely merciful, who spent their lives weeping for the spiritual and material suffering of humanity, beginning with the suffering of Adam, and invoking God's mercy. Silvanus of Mount Athos was one of these, the one to whom God one day addressed mysterious words in his affliction: "Keep your mind in hell and do not despair."[90]

But it is not only in the eschatological sense that mercy will save the world. It is the only thing that can save our present world here and now. What is the strict law that actually governs relationships between people and nations? It is still the law of retaliation, "eye for eye, tooth for tooth" (Exodus 21:24). Jesus came to break that cycle. Instead of the rule "Do to others what they do to you," he substituted the rule "Do to others what God has done to you." Through the cross Jesus "destroyed enmity" (see Ephesians 2:15-16). He destroyed enmity, not the enemy. That, by the way, is the only way to destroy the enemy. The great statesman Abraham

---

[89] Archimandrita Sofronio, *Silvano del Monte Athos. La vita, la dottrina, gli scritti* (Turin: Gribaudi, 1978), p. 195.
[90] Ibid., p. 202.

Lincoln understood this, so when someone criticized him for his excessive leniency toward his political enemies, he is said to have replied, "Do I not destroy my enemies when I make them my friends?"

It is time for us to realize that the opposite of mercy is not justice but vengeance. Jesus did not oppose mercy to justice but to the law of retaliation: "eye for eye, tooth for tooth." In forgiving sinners, God is not renouncing justice but vengeance, a desire for the death of the sinner. Instead, he takes upon himself the punishment due to sin. This is the mystery that was announced in the Old Testament and fulfilled historically in the expiatory death of Jesus.

The message we need to communicate to the world is to demythologize vengeance! Vengeance has become a pervasive mythic theme that infects everybody and everything, starting with children. The majority of films (especially the classic "Western cowboy" movies) and the stories we see on the screen, not to mention the video games that exalt vengeance, peddle it as "a victory for the good" or "the triumph of the good hero."

We have examples right in front of us to show us where the "broad" road of vengeance leads and where the "narrow" road of forgiveness and mercy leads. The law of "tit for tat" has caused the situation in the Middle East to deteriorate so much that it almost makes us lose hope about an end to the conflict in that part of the world. In contrast, Nelson Mandela, when he became part of the government, renounced vengeance against those who had kept him in prison for a good part of his life, and he achieved

not only the end of apartheid for his people but also reconciliation and peaceful coexistence for the races in South Africa. And
we have examples of the same kind right here in Italy about what
happens in feuding Mafia families when someone dares to break
the cycle and offer forgiveness.

The mercy that saves the world also saves what is the most
precious and fragile thing in the world right now: marriage and
family. What is happening to marriage is similar to what happened
in the relationship between God and humanity, as we have seen,
which the Bible in fact describes with the image of a wedding. At
the very beginning, as we have said, there was love, not mercy;
mercy arose only after humanity's rebellion. The same thing occurs
in marriage. At the beginning there is not mercy but love, often a
passionate love, between a husband and wife. But then after years
or even months of life together, the limitations of each spouse
emerge, problems of health or finance arise, and a routine sets in
. . . What can save a marriage from going downhill without any
hope of coming back again is mercy, understood in the biblical
sense we have seen, that is, not just forgiveness for offenses, but
also compassion and tenderness. *Agape* is added to *eros*, a committed, suffering love is added to erotic love, without, if possible, *eros*
being lost, since it should always continue between the spouses.

Marriage is influenced today by the current mentality of "use
it and pitch it." If a device or an instrument becomes damaged or
has a small dent, people do not think of repairing it (those who
do that work have almost disappeared) but immediately want to

replace it. People want a brand new one. When applied to marriage, this attitude is altogether mistaken and deadly. Marriage is not like a porcelain vase that can be damaged over time and never improve, and once it has a small crack loses half its worth, even if it is glued. Marriage is part of life, so it follows the law of life. How is life preserved and how does it move forward? By being kept statically in a glass case and being sheltered from shocks, changes, and atmospheric agents? Life consists of continual losses that an organism learns to repair daily, attacks by agents and viruses of every kind that an organism makes provision for and overcomes by activating its antibodies—at least until the organism is healthy. Marriage should be like wine that improves during the aging process rather than getting worse. Only mercy for one another is capable of working this miracle.

What would I suggest to spouses who would at least wish to try this path, which is demanding but full of promise? One very simple thing: rediscover a forgotten art in which our grandmothers and mothers excelled—mending! We need to substitute a "use it and mend it" mentality for the "use it and pitch it" approach. The wisest grandmothers were capable of this so-called invisible mending, performed so well that the thing seemed new and without any trace of tears. There is no need to explain what "mending the tears" of a couple means. St. Paul gives excellent advice on this issue: "Do not let the sun go down on your anger, and give no opportunity to the devil," "forbearing one another and, if one has a complaint against another, forgiving each other," and "bearing one another's burdens" (Ephesians 4:26-27; Colossians 3:13; see Galatians 6:2).

Spouses should not allow the enemy to insert a wedge between them. The important thing to understand is that in this process of rips and stitching them up, of crises and getting through them, marriage does not get damaged but grows, becomes refined, gets better. Exactly like life. The secret is in knowing how to start over from the beginning, just as life begins again every morning and at every instant, and in knowing that despite everything, it is possible to start over afresh, to wipe out the past and begin a new chapter, if both people are willing.

Jesus performed his first miracle at Cana in Galilee to save the happiness of the newlyweds. He changed water into wine, and everyone ended up agreeing that the wine that was served last was the best. I believe Jesus is still ready today, if he is invited to our marriages, to perform this miracle and make the last wine—the love and unity of the mature years of old age—better than the first.

Let us conclude by reciting Pope Francis's Prayer for the Jubilee Year of Mercy:

Lord Jesus Christ,
you have taught us to be merciful like the heavenly Father,
and have told us that whoever sees you sees Him.
Show us your face and we will be saved.
Your loving gaze freed Zacchaeus and Matthew from being
    enslaved by money;

the adulteress and Magdalene from seeking happiness only in
  created things;
made Peter weep after his betrayal,
and assured Paradise to the repentant thief.
Let us hear, as if addressed to each one of us,
  the words that you spoke to the Samaritan woman:
"If you knew the gift of God!"
You are the visible face of the invisible Father,
of the God who manifests his power above all by forgiveness
  and mercy:
let the Church be your visible face in the world, its Lord risen
  and glorified.
You willed that your ministers would also be clothed in weakness
  in order that they may feel compassion for those in ignorance
    and error:
let everyone who approaches them feel sought after, loved, and
  forgiven by God.
Send your Spirit and consecrate every one of us with
  its anointing,
so that the Jubilee of Mercy may be a year of grace
  from the Lord,
and your Church, with renewed enthusiasm, may bring good
  news to the poor,
proclaim liberty to captives and the oppressed,
and restore sight to the blind.

We ask this through the intercession of Mary,

   Mother of Mercy,

you who live and reign with the Father and the Holy Spirit

   for ever and ever.

Amen.

the WORD among us ®
The *Spirit* of Catholic Living

This book was published by The Word Among Us. Since 1981, The Word Among Us has been answering the call of the Second Vatican Council to help Catholic laypeople encounter Christ in the Scriptures.

The name of our company comes from the prologue to the Gospel of John and reflects the vision and purpose of all of our publications: to be an instrument of the Spirit, whose desire is to manifest Jesus' presence in and to the children of God. In this way, we hope to contribute to the Church's ongoing mission of proclaiming the gospel to the world so that all people would know the love and mercy of our Lord and grow ever more deeply in love with him.

Our monthly devotional magazine, *The Word Among Us*, features meditations on the daily and Sunday Mass readings, and currently reaches more than one million Catholics in North America and another half million Catholics in one hundred countries around the world. Our book division, The Word Among Us Press, publishes numerous books, Bible studies, and pamphlets that help Catholics grow in their faith.

To learn more about who we are and what we publish, log on to our website at www.wau.org. There you will find a variety of Catholic resources that will help you grow in your faith.

Embrace His Word, Listen to God . . .